Solidarity and Dissent

Union Member Attitudes
and the Political Process

by

Peter Keisler

ABOUT THE AUTHOR

PETER KEISLER currently attends Yale Law School and expects to receive his J.D. in 1985. He was awarded a B.A. in political science from Yale University in 1981. He once was a member of two unions—the Screen Actors Guild and the American Federation of Television and Radio Artists—which are affiliated with the AFL-CIO.

The Institute for Government and Politics

Stuart Rothenberg, Director, Political Division
Patrick B. McGuigan, Director, Direct Democracy Division

Board of Advisors
Jeffrey Bell, Citizens for America
Douglas R. Boyd, Director of Political Affairs, Getty Oil Company
Newt Gingrich, Member of Congress, Georgia
William F. Harvey, Carl M. Gray Professor of Law, Indiana University
Richard Woodward, President, Woodward and McDowell

The Free Congress Research and Education Foundation

Officers and Board
Kathleen Teague, Chairman
Dr. Charles Moser, Treasurer
Margaret Johnson, Secretary
Dr. Robert J. Billings
Senator William L. Armstrong
William Marshner
Michelle Laxalt

Foundation Staff
Paul M. Weyrich, President
Connaught Marshner, Executive Vice-President
Eric Licht, Vice-President for Operations
Laurie Ramsey, Vice-President for Development
John Grecco, Comptroller

Table of Contents

"Solidarity requires, not blind submission to command, but the free and timely exchange of views in search of consensus. Once that is gotten, it then requires of all the character and forbearance to defer one's own pride or preference to the general good. . . . As we go forth . . . solidarity remains the indispensable key to the future."

—Lane Kirkland, President
of the AFL-CIO, speaking at
its 14th Constitutional
Convention in New York, on
November 16, 1981

Preface

This monograph grew out of a desire to examine the tensions generated by the cross-cutting political tendencies within the contemporary American labor movement. In the 1980 presidential election, an unprecedented number of union members voted for the Republican nominee. In spite of—or because of—this, organized labor became more deeply involved in the 1984 presidential election—on behalf of a Democratic candidate—than ever before. The paradox presented seemed worthy of more detailed scrutiny than it has received thus far.

While the questions and answers in our poll were of course a partial reflection of the issues and personalities particularly relevant to this election year, we believe that the themes that emerged will be relevant and significant for years to come, as will the potential for division between the leadership and the membership of organized labor.

I would like to thank Paul Weyrich, the President of the Free Congress Foundation, for conceiving of and supporting this project. The respect and admiration he feels for the working men and women of this country are familiar to all of us who are his friends. Dr. Stuart Rothenberg was of enormous help throughout, in helping both to design the poll and interpret the results, as well as in the actual writing and organization of this monograph. The poll is the product of the high level of expertise and professionalism consistently brought to the Foundation's survey projects by Lance Tarrance and Associates. Particular thanks go to my Smith-Corona 2200, for its invaluable assistance in the typing of this manuscript.

Preface

Introduction

It was the problem that most persistently dogged Walter Mondale in his efforts to secure his party's presidential nomination—the perception, fair or unfair, that he was the candidate of the "special interests." Those who voiced this concern generally had in mind one "special interest" in particular, and at media interviews and public appearances the question was asked over and over again—"Are you too closely tied to organized labor?" The candidate's answer always began the same way: "I am proud to have the support of the working men and women of this country. . . ."

Walter Mondale's desire in the course of public discussion to transmute an endorsement from the AFL-CIO into the support of millions of American workers is understandable. The public reputation of labor unions is close to an all-time low. An ABC News/*Washington Post* survey conducted in January of 1982 found 55% of the general public endorsing the proposition that unions have too much influence, with six out of ten believing that union leaders have lost touch with the voters they represent.[1] Seymour Martin Lipset and William Schneider reported in *Public Opinion* the year before that organized labor is one of our least trusted institutions, and wrote that "there is considerable evidence that labor stands lower in public regard than business, and in some cases it is held in even lower esteem than government or politics."[2]

Many of the most important players in the American political process are organizations that in some sense represent significant numbers of voters, and their credibility and influence depend in large part on the perceived validity of their claims of representation. The AFL-CIO, at different times, has described its role in a variety of ways. It has claimed to represent its members; it has claimed to represent the interests of all working people; and it has claimed to represent the public interest broadly understood. Walter Mondale, in answering as he did, was explicitly endorsing the second view, and implicitly the third.

The monograph seeks to analyze the narrowest of these three claims of representation, through discussion of the results of a survey of 1000 randomly contacted union members all eighteen years of age or older. The poll was an extensive one, and the union members surveyed were asked their attitudes on a variety of political candidates and political issues, and on their unions and unions generally.

Organized labor is today going through a difficult period, making this study especially timely. Union organization is still substantial; there are over 150 national unions (several, like the Teamsters and the National Education Association, outside the AFL-CIO), composed of about 60,000 locals and 200,000 bargaining units, broken down into thousands of regions, districts, councils, departments and joint boards.[3] However, despite the large number of distinct unions, organized labor today is in fact thoroughly dominated by a small number of geographically concentrated larger unions. Forty-eight unions have each over 100,000 members—and they account for 88.8% of total union membership.[4] Three states, New York, California and Pennsylvania—contain one-third of all American union members, and when you throw in Ohio, Michigan and Illinois you pass the halfway mark.[5] There are large sections of this country in which union power is virtually non-existent.

And all the indices of union strength are down. Union membership has slid from 35% of the workforce in the 1940's to 25.2% in 1968 and 20.9% in 1980.[6] The private sector share is down to about 16% of the labor force; it is only because of the growth of public-sector unionism that organized labor hits 20% overall.[7] The absolute numbers continue to decline as well. Membership in unions affiliated with the AFL-CIO has fallen from 14.9 million in 1980 to 13.7 million; the Teamsters, the largest labor union, has lost approximately 400,000 members since 1979 and the United Mine Workers lost 45,000 members in 1982 alone.[8]

These numbers do not seem likely to change direction in the near future. Unions now are losing more than half of the NLRB representation elections. In 1965, labor won 60.2% of the elections held to organize non-union shops; by 1980, that figure had dropped to 45.4%.[9] To make matters even worse for organized labor, the victory figures refer disproportionately to victories in small businesses. William N. Cooke, Chairman of the Industrial Relations Program at Purdue University, recently published a study of 8,000 union certification elections in 1979, and reported that in firms with fewer than twenty employees, about 56% of the workers voted for representation and unions won 53% of the time, while in firms with between one hundred and five hundred workers, only 42% of the employees voted for representation and the unions won only 27% of the elections.[10] Many of the unions that used to be most successful are in decline. The coal miners union now represents only half of its jurisdiction, with increasing portions of the mining business going to non-union strip mines out west. The autoworkers union is reeling from the effect of foreign competition on the American automobile industry, and steelworkers are suffering a slump as well. As AFL-CIO economist John Zalusky told the *Washington Post*, "We've been losing a lot, and it hurts.[11]"

The only set of union statistics going up are those measuring political participation. In 1976, it was estimated that unions contributed $3,222,155 to Senate candidates and $2,449,170 to House candidates, and these figures did *not* include "in kind" contributions—manpower, mailings, etc.—which may have been worth nine or ten times what was spent in cash.[12] The Federal Election Commission reported that in the 1981-82 election season, organized labor contributed $5,170,526 to Senate candidates and $15,706,066 to House candidates.[13] At its recent anniversary convention, the AFL-CIO voted to boost its members' monthly dues from 19 cents to 24 cents in 1982, and 27 cents in 1983, with the receipts—an expected 14 million dollars—to be earmarked to support political candidates and to improve the image of organized labor.[14] Perhaps most significant was the decision by the AFL-CIO to endorse a candidate for the Democratic presidential nomination. The organization thus overturned a longstanding tradition of waiting until after the nomination to make or not make an endorsement, a policy that had reflected a desire to increase the likelihood of choosing a winner, to avoid being forced to choose among allies, and to prevent the AFL-CIO from becoming too closely bound up with one of the political parties. In setting that policy aside, Lane Kirkland brought involvement by organized labor in presidential politics to a new level, and made organized labor itself a central issue in the presidential campaign.

Americans hold to two contradictory images of the American laborer. On the one hand, there is a popular presumption—disputed by many pollsters—that conservative political ideology draws support predominantly from the wealthy, and liberal ideology from the working class and the poor. (The middle, as always, being up for grabs.) Hence the worker is viewed as part of a large political movement closely identified with the visions of Franklin Roosevelt and Hubert Humphrey.

At the same time, the most widely shared stereotype in our culture of the individual blue-collar worker is not Eugene V. Debs, but Archie Bunker—ignorant, politically conservative colored with a strain of bigotry, ultimately likeable but not in the least respectable. The protestors of the Sixties found that their endless seminar discussions of the great student-worker alliance had not prepared them for the "hardhats" and "rednecks," who as a group were probably more opposed to the political and cultural changes being demanded than any other economic class in the country.

In fact, the only absolutely safe generalization to make about union members is that they all belong to labor unions. The category embraces a wide range of teachers, steelworkers, government officials, secretaries, actors and truckdrivers. They are by no means monolithic in their views, and someone seeking to make predictions about the political makeup of an unknown individual might find data about that individual's gender, ethnicity, educational background and wealth all more useful than the fact that he was or was not a member of a labor union. This makes a great deal of sense; after all, while people join the Sierra Club or the Moral Majority in order to make a political statement, they generally pay dues to a labor union in order to seek improvement in their terms of employment, or simply because they must in order to keep their jobs. The aggregate responses we received to our poll were interesting, but the diversity they revealed even more so, and thus where possible we have indicated how various subgroups within our overall sample differed in their responses to our questions. It is our hope that this monograph will make a contribution to the general understanding of the role played in politics by both workers and their representative institutions, and of the relationship between the two.

Chapter 1
Attitudes About Issues

Economic Issues

We began the poll by asking those surveyed to name the problem of greatest concern to them personally:

> "In your own words, what is the number one problem facing you today—that is, what is the problem that you and your family are most concerned about?"

It was an open-ended question, with no suggested answers, and the overwhelming majority—80.6%—named an *economic* problem of some sort, such as taxes, unemployment, the cost of living, or interest rates. Only 4.8% listed a social or moral concern—such as education or crime—and 4.3% identified a concern relating to foreign policy or national defense. (See Table 1)

These were the predictable results of a question focused specifically on problems facing the respondent and his family. Were those polled asked instead to identify the most significant problems facing the *country*, for example, the answers would probably have been somewhat different. With the question worded as it was, respondents' attentions were turned to those problems most affecting *them*, and more distant concerns—like foreign policy—were less relevant. (In addition, we introduced our poll by informing the respondents that "we're talking to people all over the country today about unions and other issues facing our country," and that may have led many to assume that we were focusing on economic matters.)

There were significant differences among those polled, however, over *which* economic issues were central. Unemployment and job-related issues were named by 24.1%. Approximately 17.5% made general references to finances and money, and 29.8% cited taxes, the cost of living, or interest rates. As might be expected, those who had themselves recently been unemployed—or face the greatest risk of future unemployment—were most likely to name unemployment and job security as their primary concern, and those concerns were substantially less significant among the others. Twenty percent of our sample had been laid off at some point during the last year, 44% of them for six months or more. Of those who had been laid off for more than half of the last year, 46.7% cited job issues

Table 1. Number One Problem

	Percentage Response
Don't Know/No Answer	3.42
Unemployment	10.40
Job Security	9.97
Finances/Money	16.52
Wages/Income	7.26
Inflation	5.98
Cost of Living	7.26
Economy	5.70
No Problems	6.13
Nuclear Issues/War	3.13
Taxes	2.42
Interest Rates	1.14
Union Issues/Strikes	2.85
Government Leadership	1.99
Government Spending/Deficits	1.14
Crime	1.85
Personal/Family Health	1.42
Reduced Benefits	1.00
Retirement Concerns	1.00
Education/Teachers	0.71
Family/Children/Moral	1.71
Health Care/Cost	1.00
Breaking Unions	0.57
The Future	0.43
World Issues	1.14
Working Conditions	0.28
Social Issues	0.57
Foreign Policies/Trade	0.57
Deregulation	0.28
Environment/Ecology	0.57
Special Mentions	0.71
Other	0.85

when asked their number one problem, compared to 33.3% of those who had been laid off for less than six months and 20.4% of those who had not been laid off at all.

Similarly, those *categories* of union members that had experienced higher than average unemployment were more likely to express concern over job issues. Thus, 30.2% of the AFL-CIO members and 25.5% of the Teamsters surveyed cited job issues, while only 12.7% of government employees (a category that for our purposes excludes teachers) and 8.6% of those in education-related unions did the same. The greatest concern with unemployment was expressed by upper blue-collar workers (skilled)—35.1%—a significantly higher figure than that for either lower blue-collar workers or upper or lower white-collar workers. Similarly, as the education of those polled went up, their concern with unemployment went down. While 30.2% of those who had not finished high school were concerned about unemployment, it was cited by only 12.6% of those who had done post-graduate work. It is not only that respondents in these categories are *themselves* more likely to have been unemployed. Perhaps more importantly, they have seen more friends laid off, and have felt themselves vulnerable. Unemployment is a daily worry not only for those who are unemployed but also for those who fear they might soon be. The respondents as a whole, however, were much more likely to name general cost-of-living issues—taxes, interest rates, finances—than they were un-employment or job security. This question was asked during a period of declining unemployment. Presumably, were unemployment to rise, the number of workers in fear of losing their jobs would rise, and unemploy-ment would be cited more frequently as a primary problem.

We asked the following question:

> "Suppose that for budgeting and economic reasons, the leaders of this country have to (1) raise federal income taxes, or (2) cut federal programs and services, or (3) continue to borrow money, thus increasing our federal budget deficit. If you could tell leaders *not* to do only *one* of these, which would it be? In other words, which of these do you *dislike* the most?"

Politicians, of course, do not face this stark a choice. They may adopt more than one of these policies, and President Reagan has done all three. All the major presidential candidates oppose the high budget deficit, yet all are willing to tolerate *some* deficit. Nevertheless, there exists a powerful difference in emphasis. President Reagan has relied most heavily on economic growth and cuts in domestic spending to bring the deficit down, while Democrats who oppose his budget cuts talk in terms of tax increases. (While Walter Mondale opposes the President's defense program, he himself supports a modest increase in defense spending.)

In our sample, 34.6% were *most opposed* to continuing to borrow money; 32.9% disliked raising income taxes the most, and cutting federal pro-grams was the least unpopular alternative, with only 28.8% naming it the worst choice of the three.

There were sharp differences among categories of respondents. Those in education unions responded completely contrary to the sample gener-ally; 37.5% most opposed cutting programs, 31.3% were most against higher taxes, and only 26.6% named continued borrowing as the worst choice. In contrast, 37.1% of the AFL-CIO members named continued borrowing the least acceptable, 33.8% were most opposed to raising taxes, and only 24.8%—four percentage points lower than the aggregate—said that cutting programs was their most disliked alternative. Younger union members, aged 18-24, were less likely than most to dislike cutting programs, while 42.9% of union members 65 or older cited that as the worst alternative, perhaps reflecting concerns about social security. Black union members were significantly more opposed to cutting programs than white union members. (See Table 2)

Table 2.

Which do you *Dislike* the Most?

	Raise Taxes	Cut Fed Prog and Serv.	Continue to Borrow	Don't Know/ No Answer
White Catholic	34.8	31.0	31.0	3.2
White Protestant	30.9	28.2	37.6	3.4
White Other	31.9	19.1	40.4	8.5
Black	32.1	37.2	28.2	2.6
All Others	42.2	28.9	28.9	0.0

As the respondents move from upper white-collar down to lower blue-collar, and from higher to lower educational background, opposition to higher taxes increased while opposition to cutting programs decreased. For example, while 25.4% and 25.6%, respectively, of those without a high school diploma and those with only a high school diploma named cutting programs as the most disliked alternative, 37.0% of those with only a college diploma and 41.1% of those who have done post-graduate work did the same. (See Table 3)

The positions taken on these issues by the union organizations most aptly reflect the responses received from the well-educated, white-collar workers. Since the 1980 election in particular, organized labor has directed a great deal of energy towards opposing cutbacks in federal programs and services, while strongly supporting tax increases. In his testimony before the Democratic Party Platform Committee, AFL-CIO vice-president John H. Lyons sharply opposed the recent budget cut-backs.[1] Lane Kirkland, in a recent interview, commented, "I do not subscribe to the notion that the problem we face has anything to do with the so-called entitlements."[2] The *AFL-CIO News* is unrelenting in its criticism of President Reagan's budget, reporting, for example, that "under President Reagan, millions of Americans have dropped below the poverty line—or have been pushed below. Job and training programs

Table 3.

Which do you *Dislike* the Most?

	Raise Taxes	Cut Fed Prog and Serv.	Continue to Borrow	Don't Know/ No Answer
Upper White-Collar	28.6	32.7	35.2	3.6
Lower White-Collar	31.6	27.4	38.9	2.1
Upper Blue-Collar	36.4	25.6	34.3	3.7
Lower Blue-Collar	37.4	26.8	32.5	3.3
Less than High School	33.3	25.4	34.9	6.3
High School Graduate	39.6	25.6	32.2	2.6
Some College	26.7	24.4	43.3	5.6
College Graduate	28.3	37.0	34.8	0.0
Post Graduate Work	29.5	41.1	24.2	5.3

have been slashed 28%, unemployment insurance has been cut back, food stamp help reduced, children denied school lunches and social security slashed."[3] In fact, of the seventeen Senate votes used by the AFL-CIO to rate Senators as friendly or unfriendly to organized labor, twelve were votes on federal programs—job programs, aid to education, public works projects, and so on—with the "right" vote in each case being a vote in *favor* of the program.[4] In addition, organized labor has fought the proposed Balanced Budget Amendment from the start as "wrong in principle."[5]

Thus, while frequently expressing strong concern over growing budget deficits, the AFL-CIO has *not* supported any cutbacks in domestic social welfare programs. Instead, the Executive Council adopted a statement at its meeting in the winter of 1984 urging that the deficit be reduced through "stronger economic growth, increased federal revenues, and lower military expenditures."[6] Union opposition to reductions in income tax rates has been particularly persistent; Kirkland labeled the first Reagan tax bill "the give-away tax cut of '81," and called it "the most irresponsible fiscal act in the history of this country."[7] The AFL-CIO supports repeal of the tax cuts,[8] and Kirkland recently stated " . . . no matter who is elected, there's going to have to be a tax bill. Taxes are going to have to be raised."[9]

The opponents of President Reagan's budget cuts and tax cuts have generally couched their arguments in terms of class division: the budget cuts hurt lower-income Americans, the tax cuts favor the wealthy. That rhetoric is made more credible by the opposition of the labor movement, which has framed its rhetoric in similar terms and which speaks as the representative of the working class. Yet according to our survey, that representation on these issues is open to serious question. There was more resistance to raising taxes than cutting programs, and that generally only changed when the survey reached the upper white-collar and best-educated segment. Political candidates seeking the endorsement of organized labor would do well to support tax increases and oppose budget cuts; those that seek the votes of union members might be better off doing the reverse.

One economic policy debate in which the views of organized labor *do* seem to strongly reflect the views of the rank-and-file is that over domestic content legislation. Our poll asked:

> "Some people in this country are considering a law which would require that cars and manufactured goods sold in this country would have to contain a certain percentage of American made parts. From what you know now, do you favor or oppose this type of domestic content law?"

Fully 74.6% of our sample indicated their support for such legislation. We then asked those who indicated support a follow-up question, to present the standard counterargument and see to what extent support weakened:

> "What if you knew that this type of law would mean that the prices you pay for cars and manufactured products would go up? Would you still favor this type of law or not?"

Fully 83.4% *of those who initially favored* domestic content legislation remained in favor. Only 13.5% switched to "oppose," and 3.1% had become unsure. The Secretary of Commerce has warned that this legislation would cost American consumers an additional $1000 per automobile.[10] Supporters of the legislation dispute these figures, but our poll suggests that the debate over these consequences is largely irrelevant. Those who oppose domestic content laws will not be able to sway many working class voters by pointing to the spectre of higher prices; that is a societal and personal cost fully 62.2% (.834 × 74.6) of our sample was willing to bear. Some of the groups showing significantly higher percentages of switches, i.e., those respondents changing position after the follow-up and therefore most open to persuasion, were the young (23.1% of the respondents ages 18-24 first favored, then opposed), the poor (17.1% of those earning under $10,000 a year changed), the lower blue-collar workers (15.4% changed) those without a high school diploma (20.6% changed) and blacks (26.1% changed). Some of these groups included a disproportionate share of the less well-educated of our sample, and it may simply be that they were less familiar initially with the argument that domestic content laws lead to price increases, and needed to hear it suggested. Many of these groups, nevertheless, still had hard-core support equal in number to those in the survey generally; they just started out with fewer opposed.

Support for domestic content was particularly strong among Teamsters (75.0% favoring after the follow-up) and particularly weak among educators and government employees, with 29.5% and 26.3% respectively, initially opposing it, and an additional 9.0% and 8.8%, respectively, opposing it after the follow-up. Younger union members tended to be more opposed—only 50.8% of those 18-24 favored the legislation after the follow-up—and those who had been unemployed during the last year were significantly more supportive. Union activists—those who have served or currently serve in union offices or on union committees—were more likely by about five percentage points than non-activists to support domestic content laws, and in general the wealthier, upper white-collar, better educated workers were most opposed. This is an issue on which official union positions match those of the members. Organized labor not only supports domestic content, it has lobbied for it vigorously.[11] In doing so, it seems to have the strong support of the rank-and-file.

Defense Spending

Defense spending had always been an area in which organized labor and the community of liberal Democrats parted company. Part of this, of course, was attributable to the large number of unions whose members are dependent for work on defense contracts, but even more significant was the fierce anti-communism of one man. It was George Meany who was responsible for the statement by the AFL-CIO Executive Council in 1966 that not only supported President Johnson's efforts in Vietnam, but also attacked "those who would deny our military forces unstinting support (and) are, in effect, aiding the Communist enemy of our country."[12] And it was George Meany who in testifying before the Senate Foreign Relations Committee in 1974 called detente "a one-way street in which the Soviet Union maintains all its political objectives which are fundamentally antagonistic to the West, while it acquires from the West the technology it needs to help overcome the disastrous economic consequences of totalitarian economic planning.[13] Jesse Helms never talked tougher.

With Meany's death, the firm support for defense programs that he built into the AFL-CIO has not dissolved, but cracks are beginning to show. Thus, Lane Kirkland, asked recently about the position of the U.S. Chamber of Commerce in favor of cutting the defense budget, re-

sponded, "I regard that as a further demonstration that the business and
financial community of this country is the soft underbelly of freedom."[14]
However, while the AFL-CIO has, for example, reaffirmed its support for
the MX missile, the United Food and Commerical Workers Union, the
Machinists, and the American Federation of State, County and Municipal
Employees have all lobbied against it, and some more liberal Federation
staffers upset with their employer's position have come to label the
organization the "AFL-CIA."[15] In 1981, the AFL-CIO Executive Council
merely complained that *simultaneously* cutting domestic spending and
increasing defense spending would undermine public support for defense, and urged the Reagan Administration to maintain spending for
both; in 1982, however, the Executive Council explicitly questioned the
Reagan increase, charging that the $33 billion would be "taken out of the
hides of the poor."[16]

This represents a shift in rhetoric as well as in labor's official position,
but its political impact is unlikely to be significant. Although organized
labor has often lobbied in support of defense programs, its election
endorsements and contributions almost never reflect these positions.
COPE ratings are compiled without reference to a single defense vote,
and much of labor's strongest support goes to those members of Congress, such as Senators Howard Metzenbaum (D-Ohio), Donald Riegle (D-
Mich) and Alan Cranston (D-Calif), who take positions on defense most
diametrically opposed to those of the AFL-CIO.

Among union members in our survey, we found a signficant variation in
opinion. Overall, there was more opposition than support for increased
defense spending. (See Table 4)

Table 4. Defense Spending

	Percentage Response
Increase/Strongly	23.0
Increase	8.5
Unsure	15.2
Decrease	12.1
Decrease/Strongly	37.0
Don't Know/No Answer	4.2

When we broke the numbers down, we saw many of the same patterns we
had seen in other questions. Teamsters were more supportive of defense
spending than others, and those in education unions and government
employee unions significantly less so. (See Table 5)

Table 5. Defense Spending

	Increase	Unsure	Decrease
AFL-CIO	33.7	19.0	47.3
Teamsters	43.4	15.8	40.8
Education/Schools	24.1	17.5	58.4
Government Related	21.3	27.5	51.3

The more liberal and Democratic a respondent identified himself as, the more likely he was to strongly favor decreasing the amount spent on defense. The more educated tended to favor reducing the defense budget. The class of union members most supportive of increasing defense were the upper blue-collar workers. (See Table 6)

Table 6. Defense Spending

	Increase	Unsure	Decrease
Upper White Collar	25.0	17.0	58.0
Lower White-Collar	34.8	17.8	47.4
Upper Blue-Collar	36.2	20.4	43.4
Lower Blue-Collar	30.8	20.9	48.4

The male/female differences that have shown up in national polls on this issue showed up in ours as well. While 25.9% of the men strongly favored a defense increase, only 17.9% of the women took that position, and while 34.8% of the men strongly favored a decrease, among women the figure was 40.8%. There were significant differences among ethnic and racial groups as well. (See Table 7)

Table 7. Defense Spending

	Increase	Unsure	Decrease
White Catholic	32.8	21.3	45.8
White Protestant	38.0	18.9	43.1
White Other	25.6	18.0	56.4
Black	15.3	19.8	64.9

Interestingly, the gap that so often appeared between union activists and non-activists was *not* present in response to this question—the differences were quite marginal. Overall, the data suggest simply that there is significant division among union members on this question, with more supporting decreases in defense spending. Whatever the movement over time, organized labor is unlikely to ever beome a vigorous opponent of defense spending; but they will help elect quite a few.

Education

We queried our respondents on two education issues: tuition tax credits and teacher competency tests. In each case, the responses from teachers set them apart from the sample as a whole.

We asked:

"Do you favor or oppose a tuition tax credit—where parents are given tax credits if they choose to send their children to private or parochial schools?"

A plurality of our sample opposed tuition tax credits. (See Table 8)

Table 8. Tuition Tax Credits

	Percentage Response
Favor	44.6
Unsure	6.3
Oppose	48.9
Don't Know/No Answer	0.2

The margin between supporters and opponents was signficantly higher among union activists. (See Table 9)

Table 9. Tuition Tax Credits

	Favor	Unsure	Oppose
Union Activists	41.8	5.6	52.6
Non-Activists	45.8	6.9	47.3

The most marked opposition came from teachers. More Teamsters and government employees favored than opposed. (See Table 10)

Table 10. Tuition Tax Credits

	Favor	Unsure	Oppose
AFL-CIO	44.7	7.5	47.8
Teamsters	48.7	7.9	43.4
Education/Schools	36.1	4.2	59.6
Government Related	48.8	5.0	46.3

These figures are mirrored by the strong opposition among teacher unions. While the AFL-CIO has officially opposed tuition tax credits, it has been the teachers unions that have most vocally and actively fought the concept. They have argued that tuition tax credits would destroy the public school system, by encouraging widespread flight into private schools. The assumption upon which this conclusion is implicitly premised is that the only thing keeping many students in the public schools is the fact that the alternatives are unaffordable; given the financial capability, it is assumed, lower income students would choose to leave the public school system. Many statistics bear this out, particularly the high percentages of minority studens in Catholic parochial schools. (In 1976, it was estimated that 60% of the students at Catholic schools in the New York archdiocese were black or Hispanic.)

We found that a majority of the poorest among our sample—the lower white-collar and the lower blue-collar workers—supported tuition tax credits. (See Table 11)

Table 11. Tuition Tax Credits

	Favor	Unsure	Oppose
Upper White-Collar	38.6	5.3	56.1
Lower White-Collar	51.9	8.1	40.0
Upper Blue-Collar	44.5	5.5	50.0
Lower Blue-Collar	50.5	7.7	41.8

It is the least wealthy for whom tuition tax credits might make the most difference; for them, tuition tax credits might mean the difference between being able to send their children to a private school and being unable to do so. The offical labor policy runs squarely against their view.

We next asked about competency tests:

"Do you favor or oppose requiring teachers in this country to pass competency tests in order to continue to teach in the public schools?"

There was overwhelming support. (See Table 12)

Table 12. Competency Tests

	Percentage Response
Favor	82.6
Unsure	3.1
Oppose	14.1
Don't Know/No Answer	0.2

Union activists were significantly less supportive. (See Table 13)

Table 13. Competency Tests

	Favor	Unsure	Oppose
Union Activists	78.1	2.3	19.6
Non-Activists	84.7	3.7	11.6

Once again, educators responded in a strikingly different way, although *even among educators* a majority *supported* competency tests. (See Table 14)

Table 14. Competency Tests

	Favor	Unsure	Oppose
AFL-CIO	91.0	1.9	7.1
Teamsters	83.0	6.4	10.6
Education/Schools	54.7	3.1	42.2
Government Related	92.1	3.2	4.8

Thus, the position many education unions have taken on competency tests does not reflect the position of a majority of their members.

It is nevertheless true that *more* teachers tend to be opposed to tuition tax credits and competency tests than do other union members. What is interesting is the way the positions of teachers unions on education issues have come to be the positions of so many other unions, such as the AFL-CIO (to which the American Federation of Teachers belong), despite the fact that the views of the members of teachers unions are so strikingly distinctive when compared with the views of other union members.

Individual Rights Issues

The history of organized labor's relationship with the black community has its ugly moments. Many unions as originally constituted were expressly racist, and worked, often with great success, to drive blacks out of the workforce. As one commentator wrote:

"In Philadelphia in 1838, the Society of Friends had compiled a directory of occupations in which Negroes [freemen] were employed. Significantly included were such skilled jobs as cabinetmaker, plumber, printer, sailmaker, ship's carpenter, stonecutter, and many others. By the end of the 1890's, Negroes had been forced out of both these and other craft occupations. . . . In the older seaboard cities of the South, Negroes had once been employed in a great variety of occupations, skilled and unskilled.

> However, in the last decades of the 19th century, the process of Negro displacement had begun, and trade unions were a most important part of this development. . . . In both South and North, the trade union opposes black labor wherever it can and admits into fellowship only as a last resort."[17]

Since black workers were willing to accept lower wages, they were seen as "stealing" jobs from whites. In 1909, for example, a bitter strike action was taken by the Brotherhood of Locomotive Firemen against Georgia Railroad, in which the union demanded that all blacks be taken off the road. The settlement in the end provided that blacks and whites would be paid the same, and a union spokesman responded, "If this course is followed by the company and the incentive for employing Negroes thus removed, the strike will not have been in vain."[18] In fact, throughout the South in the railroad industry, skilled jobs like fireman, brakeman and switchman had been filled with blacks in the late nineteenth and early twentieth century; with the growth of unionization, the numbers declined dramatically.[19] Samuel Gompers, regarded as the founder of the American trade union movement, once put it this way: "Caucasions are not going to let their standard of living be destroyed by Negroes, Chinamen, Japs or any others."

That history is past, but it illustrates the tension that did and does exist between unions and the unskilled poor. Approximately 14% of union members in America are black.[20] At the same time, the unskilled poor—a class in which blacks are disproportionately represented—are competitors with union members for jobs, and the fear of being underbid is a real one.

The present record of organized labor on race issues is therefore a confusing blend. On the one hand, the American trade union movement is allied with many major organizations prominent in the civil rights community, and they have fought shoulder to shoulder in many legislative battles. The AFL-CIO has even given direct financial support to these organizations; for example, when an Alabama judge demanded a punitive bond from the NAACP in 1975, the AFL-CIO provided over half the money.[21] Although in the early seventies the AFL-CIO fought bitterly against racial quotas for delegate selection at the Democratic Conventions,[22] the organization has more recently taken strong and public positions in favor of affirmative action. Delegates to the AFL-CIO convention last October adopted a resolution which declared, "We strongly advocate that the federal government abandon its retreat from affirmative action efforts."[23] AFL-CIO officials have criticized the President's filling of the Civil Rights Commission and the Equal Employment

Opportunity Commission with "people who see no virtue in affirmative action,"[24] and Lane Kirkland issued a similar criticism at the celebration of the 75th anniversary of the NAACP.[25]

Nevertheless, while organized labor has allied itself with the civil rights community on broad, general issues, whenever positions favored by that community threaten to directly endanger union jobs, the tone shifts. In recent public employee cases in which seniority systems were disrupted in order to avoid laying off less-senior black workers hired under court-ordered affirmative action plans, unions backed maintenance of seniority rights. The youth sub-minimum wage proposal of the Reagan Administration, endorsed by the Conference of Black Mayors as a way of spurring minority youth unemployment, is bitterly opposed by union officials who fear being underbid. The result of their successful opposition has been to price the least-skilled workers out of the labor market, reminiscent in some ways of the results of the railway strike mentioned earlier. The Enterprise Zone proposal, sponsored by Congressman Robert Garcia (a Democrat who represents the burnt-out South Bronx in New York) has been attacked by the trade unions. And the recently contested Simpson-Mazzoli immigration bill, opposed passionately by the vast majority of black and Hispanic congressmen who feared that imposing sanctions on employers who hire illegal aliens would lead to job discrimination, was strongly supported by organized labor, which feared cheap labor somewhat more. The one provision of the bill supported by minority groups—the granting of amnesty to illegals already in the country—was the provision that the AFL-CIO opposed in a separate letter to every member of Congress. It was in the context of these tensions that Jesse Jackson predicted that a black or female would become President of the United States before someone besides a white male headed the AFL-CIO.[26]

"Affirmative action" is a term that connotes different things to different people. Some who say they support it mean that they support affirmative attempts to recruit members of minority groups. Others go further, and support numerical racial quotas, or rhetorically softer but indistinguishable "goals" and "timetables." We first asked our respondents the following question:

> "Do you personally favor or oppose government affirmative action programs to ensure that blacks, Hispanics, women and other minorities are not discriminated against in the workforce?"

The focus was simply on ending discrimination, and defined in those terms, affirmative action won strong support, with 72.1% favorable. (See Table 15)

Table 15. Affirmative Action to Ensure No Discrimination

	Percentage Response
Favor	72.1
Unsure	6.4
Oppose	20.7

We then asked a follow-up question *only* to those who had indicated in response to the last question that they *favored* affirmative action:

"And what if you knew that these affirmative action programs would give minority group members special treatment in hiring and promotion within companies? Would you still favor affirmative action programs or not?"

More than half of those initially in favor switched sides. (See Table 16)

Table 16. Affirmative Action as Special Treatment

	Percentage Response (out of the 721 respondents who initially favored)
Yes/Still Favor	36.3
Unsure	7.9
No/Now Oppose	54.9
Don't Know/No Answer	0.8

Thus, *only 36.3% of those surveyed favored affirmative action if affirmative action implied favoring members of any racial or ethnic group in hiring.* Whether or not explicit quotas are used, the vast majority of those surveyed *opposed* the taking of race or ethnicity into account when hiring decisions are made.

There were stark differences among the different unions. (See Table 17)

Table 17. Affirmative Action

	Favored after Both Questions	Favored, then Opposed	Opposed	Unsure
AFL-CIO	22.2	47.8	22.5	7.5
Teamsters	35.5	39.5	19.7	5.3
Education/Schools	31.3	44.6	16.9	7.2
Government Related	25.0	46.3	20.0	8.8

Note that the Teamsters, often the most politically conservative of the labor unions, were most supportive of affirmative action after being asked the follow-up, while the members of the AFL-CIO showed the largest gap—25.6 percentage points—between the number favoring affirmative action as defined in the first question and the number favoring affirmative action as defined in the second. Twenty-eight percent of the union activists supported affirmative action after the second question, while only 25.4% of the non-activists did the same. The poorest were the least supportive—31.4% of those earning under $10,000 a year opposed affirmative action from the beginning, and only 17.1% supported it after the second question. The best educated were the most supportive. (See Table 18)

Table 18. Affirmative Action

	Favored after Both Questions	Favored, then Opposed	Opposed	Unsure
Less than High School	27.8	44.3	22.7	5.2
High School Graduate	25.6	45.2	21.8	7.4
Some College	20.0	47.3	23.7	9.0
College Graduate	32.3	48.4	12.9	6.5
Post Graduate Work	33.9	43.3	17.3	5.5

The ethnic group of respondents strongest in support of affirmative action were black union members, 50.5% of whom favored the concept in response to the second question.

The meaning of the union leadership's rhetoric on affirmative action remains unclear, perhaps by conscious design. As is, the unions give lip service to a principle important to their allies, yet maintain enough ambiguity to avoid endorsing a point of view so at odds with that of the rank and file. There is little ambiguity in the views of the membership. Politicians who talk about the need to ensure that no minority group is met with discrimination will find strong support for that position among the rank and file. Those who extend that principle to include a program that gives explicit hiring preferences to members of certain groups, however, will meet with a different reaction entirely. The responses to our questions were unambiguous—strong opposition to discrimination against members of minority groups, and strong opposition to any form of special treatment. This is in fact the position of the Reagan Justice Department, which has bucked the tide of many recent legal trends by asserting that the Constitution mandates a "colorblind" law. It is a position that has generated a great deal of controversy, but one around which a political candidate can expect to rally support among the working class.

We asked those surveyed their attitudes toward what has recently become one of the most hotly contested issues in the debate over gender discrimination: comparable worth. Comparable worth is a concept that seeks to redefine what is meant by discrimination.

Under the old view, discrimination existed when those of equal ability holding the same job received disparate salaries. Comparable worth seeks to extend that to a new level, comparing *different* jobs to see whether those doing *comparable* work are paid *comparable* wages. Comparability is determined by an outside consultant, who analyzes a particular company and uses a complicated scoring system to measure each job in terms of difficulty, educational requirements, value to the company, and so on; the consultant thus develops a scale to compare, for example, secretaries and what *they* get paid to janitors and what *they* get paid. Supporters believe it would make wages more equitable, and raise pay scales in female-dominated occupations. Opponents believe that secretaries who want the salaries of janitors can and should become janitors, and that comparable worth represents a radical attack on the foundations of free-market economics.

Organized labor leadership is strongly supportive of comparable worth, and Lane Kirkland has characterized it as "an element of simple justice."[27] The leading organized labor supporters are the government employee unions, with large numbers of female clerical workers as members. The President of the American Federation of State, County and Municipal Employees, for example, has called it "an important litmus test."[28] We found strong support among the members we surveyed.

Because the concept of comparable worth is by and large unfamiliar to most voters, we explained it in two different ways by adding a follow-up question. We first asked:

> "As you may know, some states are trying to reduce sex discrimination in the workplace with the principle of comparable pay for comparable work. In these states, a commission studies the requirements of each job, and then proposes an equal pay scale if two jobs have comparable job requirements. From what you know now, do you favor or oppose laws requiring this type of comparable pay for comparable work?"

The results were overwhelming: 88.0% favored, only 8.9% opposed. We then framed this issue in terms of the incongruities that opponents of comparable worth like to highlight, by asking *those who already said they favored* comparable worth the following:

> "What if you knew that this meant that plumbers would be paid the same as nurses, or that secretaries would be paid the same as truck drivers? Would you still favor this comparable pay law or not?"

There were some switches, but most of our respondents—59.0% of those who initially favored (51.9% of the entire sample)—*still* favored comparable worth. Of the 880 people that were asked the follow-up, 8.4% had become unsure and 32.2% switched to opposition. (See Table 19)

Table 19. Comparable Worth

	Percentage Response
First Question:	
Favor	88.0
Unsure	2.9
Oppose	8.9
Don't Know/No Answer	0.2
Second Question:	(out of the 880 who initially favored)
Yes/Still Favor	59.0
Unsure	8.4
No/Now Oppose	32.2
Don't Know/No Answer	0.4

We found especially strong support among members of government employee unions and education unions, and more opposition among members of the AFL-CIO. (See Table 20)

Table 20. Comparable Worth

	Favored after Both Questions	Favored, then Opposed	Opposed	Unsure
AFL-CIO	47.6	38.8	11.0	2.6
Teamsters	52.6	38.2	7.9	1.3
Education/Schools	65.1	27.7	4.8	2.4
Government Related	57.5	31.3	3.8	7.5

Union activists were significantly more willing to support comparable worth after the follow-up than non-activists—57.2% of the activists supported the concept, while only 49.6% of the non-activists did so. White-collar workers were more supportive than blue-collar workers, and the more educated were more supportive than the less educated. (See Table 21)

These numbers suggest that the concept of comparable worth has substantial support among union members. Clearly, identifying hypothetical incongruities that might result will lessen support somewhat, but opponents of comparable worth are going to have to develop other means of framing the issue in order to win support for their position among

Table 21. Comparable Worth

	Favored after Both Questions	Favored, then Opposed	Opposed	Unsure
Upper White-Collar	62.5	28.8	6.4	2.3
Lower White-Collar	56.3	35.6	5.9	2.2
Upper Blue-Collar	48.0	39.1	10.6	2.3
Lower Blue-Collar	45.1	38.5	12.1	4.4
Less than High School	43.3	41.2	11.3	4.1
High School Graduate	46.9	39.5	10.4	3.2
Some College	50.6	38.0	8.2	3.3
College Graduate	61.3	28.2	8.9	1.6
Post Graduate Work	67.7	26.0	3.9	2.4

union members. It might, for example, be useful for opponents to point out that under a regime of comparable worth, the steelworkers union sitting across from management at the bargaining table will find management more reluctant to increase wage scales, because whatever is put into one contract will have legally mandated repercussions for all other contracts negotiated by the same company. (In fact, the concept of comparable worth is fundamentally antithetical to that of collective bargaining, because it rejects the notion that the value of labor is defined by the outcome of negotiations between employer and employee.) Opponents might also find it useful to highlight some of the rhetoric used by supporters of comparable worth—rhetoric sometimes characterized by subtle but recognizable contempt for blue-collar manual laborers who are "unfairly" paid more than office workers. For example, Democratic Vice-Presidential nominee Geraldine Ferraro defends comparable worth in the following terms: "A woman with a college education can expect lifetime earnings equal to those paid to a man who never finished the eighth grade. Groundskeepers are paid more than nurses. Parking lot attendants are often paid more than experienced secretaries. We entrust our children our most precious resource—to teachers who frequently earn less than truck drivers."[29] But however the issue might be framed in the future, as currently defined it commands strong support not only from union leadership but from membership as well.

The final individual rights issue we included in our poll was the question of amnesty for illegal aliens, strongly supported by major civil rights organizations. As mentioned earlier, while the AFL-CIO supported the Simpson-Mazzoli immigration reform bill, it strongly opposed including the amnesty provision. The day the House voted on—and very narrowly defeated—a proposed amendment to delete the amnesty provision, every member of the House received a letter from the AFL-CIO urging them to vote in favor of the amendment.

The results of our poll indicate that this was a position generally favored by the rank and file. (See Table 22)

Table 22. Amnesty

"One part of an immigration bill being considered by Congress would make illegal aliens who have lived continuously in the U.S. for six or more years eligible for permanent resident status. Do you favor or oppose this provision of the immigration bill?"

	Percentage Response
Favor	39.5
Unsure	8.6
Oppose	50.7
Don't Know/No answer	1.3

Blue-collar workers were clearly more likely to oppose amnesty than were white-collar workers. (See Table 23)

Table 23. Amnesty

	Favor	Unsure	Oppose
Upper White-Collar	42.9	12.2	44.9
Lower White-Collar	42.1	16.8	41.1
Upper Blue-Collar	39.7	5.0	55.4
Lower Blue-Collar	33.3	10.6	56.1

This is possibly a reflection of the fact that blue-collar jobs, and not white-collar jobs, are more likely to be filled with illegal aliens.

Conclusions

The views of the leadership and the rank and file seem to be most congruent on those issues in which unions and their members see union jobs directly threatened—domestic content legislation, amnesty for illegal aliens, and seniority systems threatened by racial quotas. The quirk is defense spending, with the leadership taking positions more supportive of increased spending than the membership at large. With the exception of domestic content, which is an issue with no clearly defined ideological base, these are all issues over which the leadership of organized labor has parted company with the positions generally taken by American liberals.

As the poll moves to issues of more diffuse impact, this congruence begins to dissolve. The most striking comparison is that between leadership and membership views on economic policy; leadership supports higher taxes and opposes cutbacks in domestic spending, priorities which do not in the least reflect the views of membership. The segment of membership most supportive of leadership positions on these issues is *not* the blue-collar, less educated, lower income class, but the more wealthy, better educated, white collar class. Candidates seeking to build a blue-collar constituency seem unlikely to be successful running on a platform of increasing taxes and domestic spending. Similarly, endorsing racial preferences of any sort seems likely to alienate working class voters. On this issue, as on the economic issues, conservatives are in a position to make significant inroads on a constituency traditionally thought of as liberal.

The issue on which there was perhaps the most striking agreement between leadership and membership was the issue of comparable worth. Organized labor support for this concept is matched by support from the rank and file. The issue is currently being defined in a way that finds support among working class voters, and opponents of comparable worth will need to find other methods of framing and discussing this issue if their opposition is to be successful.

Chapter 2
Attitudes Towards Elections

"Ronald Reagan protects the sacred cows of America—the oil companies, the gas companies, the largest corporations and the rich. But the President that so many of you voted for—and you don't have to tell me which ones of you voted for him, because too damn many of you did, and you know it and I know it. . . . "[1]

—Senator Howard Metzenbaum (D-Ohio),
speaking to the United Auto Workers

Over the years, organized labor has developed sophisticated and well-financed political organizations that are involved in races at virtually every level of American politics. Since 1974, according to Common Cause, six of the ten biggest givers among political action committees have been unions: the Auto Workers (second place), the AFL-CIO (fourth), the Machinists (fifth), the Steelworkers (eighth), the National Education Association (ninth) and the Seafarers (tenth).[2] The most significant is the AFL-CIO's Committee on Political Education (COPE), formed in 1955 through a merger of the AFL's Labor League for Political Education and the CIO's Political Action Committee.

Back in 1970, the then-Director of COPE said the following:

> We're kind of proud of our organization. We've got organizations in fifty damn states and it goes right down from the states to the citizens. There's no party that can match us. Give us ten years or fifteen years and we'll have the best political organization in the history of this country.[3]

This of course was part bravado, but the pride was well-deserved. COPE was and is a significant force in our politics. After making an endorsement—and the local and state COPE's have final veto over endorsements for candidates in their regions—COPE provides financial assistance and in-kind assistance, such as voter registration drives. In areas of the country where union membership is substantial, COPE has a clear impact; in Pennsylvania, for example, over 80% of union members are registered, a figure substantially higher than normal for those of similar socio-economic status.[4] However, there are large parts of the country—the South, for example—in which COPE has very little strength, and the negative image of labor in those areas forces COPE to time its contributions so as to avoid their being publicized until after the election.[5] In addition to

COPE, there are many independent political organizations formed both by unions that belong to the AFL-CIO and unions that do not, the former having formed independent PACs in part as a result of disenchantment with COPE's neutrality in the 1972 presidential campaign.

COPE is officially bipartisan, but its always powerful ties to the Democratic Party have become even stronger in recent years. Back in 1966, George Meany declared, "I don't buy the idea, and there is nothing to sustain it, that labor needs the Democratic Party. I'm sure it is the other way around."[6] Meany conceded in a separate interview, however, that organized labor would support more Democrats than Republicans "because that probably will be just the way it works out."[7] Republican Senator Margaret Chase Smith of Maine, who scored over 80% with COPE, was bitter when her opponent received the endorsement,[8] and it was not until 1974 that COPE endorsed any Republicans in Senate races—Richard Schweiker of Pennsylvania (COPE rating 100), Jacob Javits of New York and Charles Mathias of Maryland.

Organized labor is more closely tied to the Democratic Party than it ever was, possibly because relations with the White House are colder than they have been with any recent Republican administration. In an interview on National Public Radio, COPE director John Perkins asserted, "The AFL-CIO remains politically independent and will support candidates regardless of their party affiliation. . . . While labor is not becoming a branch of the Democratic Party, it has difficulty finding Republican candidates who share its views."[9] According to figures released by the Federal Election Commission, in the 1981-82 election season, labor union PACs gave over 94% of their money to Democrats.[10] Democrats as a whole *are* much more supportive of labor's official policy positions. Congressmen scoring over 90% in COPE ratings are almost always Democrats—often Democrats with fewer than the national mean of blue-collar workers in their districts—and the correlation in 1974 between COPE ratings and those of the liberal Americans for Democratic Action was 0.84.[11]

Official organizational ties between organized labor and the Democrats are growing. Organized labor demanded and received a majority of the at-large seats on the Democratic National Committee.[12] One AFL-CIO publication made the following report of a labor gathering devoted to discussion of union involvement in the political process:

> "The 1982 delegates had numerous complaints about the political parties, particularly the Democrats: 'They want our work but don't want to give us a say. . . . The party has collapsed in our area . . . there is no party. . . . They run as Democrats but once elected they pay no attention to the party. . . .

We are shut out of the party.' But pursuit of the discussion revealed considerable change since 1980. Labor was more involved, in almost every case, than two years ago. More labor representatives had been attending state and caucus meetings, had increased representation on state and county central committees, and had the feeling Democratic Party leaders were at least beginning to listen. In a few situations, the lack of party structure resulted in labor carrying much or nearly all the burden of seeing that the party functioned."[13]

There are, of course, dissidents. The Machinists and the United Electrical Workers both called in 1980 for studying the possibility of a new, independent labor-led political party that would, in the words of a resolution from the Electrical Workers, "end the reliance on so-called friends of labor who in the crunch vote for the corporations."[14] The Teamsters and the now-defunct Professional Air Traffic Controllers Union endorsed Ronald Reagan in 1980. But by and large, the American labor union movement exercises its greatest political influence through the Democratic Party.

We asked those surveyed about their voting patterns, and whether they usually vote Democratic or Republican. If given the choice, many people will say that they are independent, and that they vote for "the man" and not the party. Therefore, we did not include that as an option, but recorded it when it was volunteered. A majority of our respondents identified themselves as Democrats. (See Table 24)

Table 24.

"Which of these statements best describes how you usually vote?"

	Percentage Response
Mostly Republican	11.7
Slightly Republican	7.7
The Man	22.6
Slightly Democratic	15.2
Mostly Democratic	39.9
Don't Know/No Answer	2.9

Teamsters were more likely than the sample as a whole to identify themselves as Republican in voting habits. So were those in education unions, 25.3% of whom sided more often with the Republican Party. This was offset, however, by the fact that educators were also more likely to identify their voting behavior as Democratic than was the sample as a whole; they compensated for these figures by being unusually unlikely to volunteer that they vote for "the man." (See Table 25)

Table 25. Voting Behavior

	Republican	The Man	Slightly Democratic	Mostly Democratic
AFL-CIO	16.8	26.0	15.4	41.8
Teamsters	27.6	34.2	7.9	30.3
Education/Schools	25.3	16.3	21.7	36.7
Government Related	16.3	32.5	13.8	37.5

There was a significant disparity between the views of activists and the views of non-activists, with activists demonstrating far greater allegiance to the Democratic Party than non-activists. (See Table 26)

Table 26. Voting Behavior

	Republican	The Man	Slightly Democratic	Mostly Democratic
Union Activists	13.8	19.7	16.4	50.0
Non-Activists	21.8	28.0	14.7	35.5

Fully 66.4% of the activists characterized their voting behavior as Democratic, while only 50.2% of non-activists so characterized *their* voting behavior. Women by a significant margin identified more closely with the Democrats. (See Table 27)

Table 27. Voting Behavior

	Republican	The Man	Slightly Democratic	Mostly Democratic
Male	19.9	29.1	14.4	36.7
Female	18.8	19.3	16.6	45.4

Despite this loyalty to the Democratic Party, opinion about Ronald Reagan was more evenly divided. We asked those surveyed:

"Do you approve or disapprove of the way Ronald Reagan is handling his job as President?"

There was more disapproval than approval, but the gap was much narrower (48.3% to 40.6%) than that between Democrats and Republicans (55.1% to 19.4%). (See Table 28)

Table 28. Ronald Reagan

	Percentage Response
Approve	40.6
Undecided	10.3
Disapprove	48.3
Don't Know/No Answer	0.8

Those who had been recently unemployed were significantly more disapproving of President Reagan. (See Table 29)

Table 29. Ronald Reagan

	Approve	Undecided	Disapprove
Unemployed for six months or more out of the last twelve	24.1	8.0	67.8
Unemployed for less than six months out of the last twelve	38.9	10.6	50.4
Not unemployed during last year	42.6	11.5	45.9

Teamsters and Educators were more approving than disapproving; AFL-CIO members and government employees were the reverse. (See Table 30)

Table 30. Ronald Reagan

	Approve	Unsure	Disapprove
AFL CIO	38.3	11.7	50.0
Teamsters	57.9	7.9	34.2
Education/Schools	46.4	11.4	42.2
Government Related	35.0	10.0	55.0

(The Teamsters supported President Reagan in 1980; the National Education Association supported Jimmy Carter, and endorsed Walter Mondale in the 1984 primaries early on.) Both white Catholics and white Protestants, taken alone, evinced more approval than disapproval. It is only after other white ethnic groups and blacks are factored in that the sample as a whole registers more disapproval. (See Table 31)

Table 31. Ronald Reagan

	Approve	Unsure	Disapprove
White Catholic	48.2	8.7	43.1
White Protestant	46.5	11.9	41.6
White Other	33.8	14.3	51.9
Black	10.8	8.1	81.1

Recent polls have shown that Ronald Reagan is drawing his strongest support among the young. Our polls support this trend as well. The younger voters were more likely to approve of his job performance. (See Table 32)

Table 32. Ronald Reagan

	Approve	Unsure	Disapprove
Ages 18-34	45.0	9.0	46.0
Ages 35-44	39.4	17.1	48.5
Ages 45-up	36.5	12.4	51.1

Of most interest was the wide gap between the views of union activists and non-activists. If the activists—those who run for union offices, or serve on union committees—were removed from our poll, the President would actually have more union members approving than disapproving of his performance. (See Table 33)

Table 33. Ronald Reagan

	Approve	Unsure	Disapprove
Union Activists	29.9	13.2	56.9
Non-Activists	45.3	10.2	44.5

This is not a startling result. Ronald Reagan won an unusually large number of normally Democratic voters in 1980. Whereas Jimmy Carter won 63% of union votes in the 1976 general election—as compared to 36% of non-union votes[15]—when Ronald Reagan ran in 1980 he won 43% of the union vote and 47% of the blue-collar vote generally.[16] In the 1980 presidential election, union leaders neither represented nor convinced a large enough number of their members. The fact that approval remains high among rank and file suggests that defections originally attributed to dislike of Jimmy Carter may in fact have found their source in positive feelings of support for Ronald Reagan.

We asked our respondents to give one or two reasons for their approval or disapproval of President Reagan's performance in office. The emphasis of those who approved was on personal qualities and general leadership. Fully 48.2% gave reasons like "doing a good job," "strong leadership," or "fulfilled promises." Approximately 29.5% mentioned economic issues, and 14.4% cited foreign policy or defense. On the other hand, those who disapproved were much less likely to focus on the President's personal qualities. Economic issues were cited by 50.7% of those who disapproved of the President, with general comments about character—"inefficient," "inexperienced," "promises not kept" and so on—made by only 18.3%. These figures suggest that while many of the President's positions may be supported by union members, it is his personal qualities that are most responsible for his appeal. This casts doubt on the permanence of union defections from the Democratic Party. These votes cannot be inherited; when Reagan retires, they will have to be won once again.

In the 1984 election season, the AFL-CIO made a break with tradition, and decided to endorse a candidate in the Democratic primaries, provided two-thirds of the one-hundred-and-forty-four member general board could agree on a choice. The two-thirds were there for Walter Mondale, and Kirkland, who had promised that the AFL-CIO would do "everything in our power" to elect a new President,[17] made a massive investment of the organization's resources and prestige. Millions were spent on rallies, brochures, and phone calls on Mondale's behalf,[18] and Kirkland even gave Mondale the most memorable line of his campaign: before the famous debate in which Mondale first uttered the phrase, Kirkland had given a speech on Senator Gary Hart's "new ideas" and asked "Where's the beef?"

Union help was particularly important in Alabama, Michigan, Illinois, New York and Pennsylvania. In fact, 51% of Mondale's vote in Pennsylvania came from union households.[19] Democratic campaign consultant Robert Squier doubted that Mondale would ever have won without the union support; Mondale campaign manager Robert Beckel merely commented, "We could have won without organized labor, but it would have been a lot more difficult."[20]

The relationship Walter Mondale built with organized labor was not, however, an unmixed blessing. A labor meeting in Los Angeles responded enthusiastically to Mondale's call to "elect someone who will remember who put him there,"[21] but to others statements like that were a source of unease. According to an ABC News exit poll, Hart's perceived freedom from interest groups was a major reason for his victory in the New Hampshire primary, and Mondale may have lost 20% of the vote as a result.[22] An exit poll by NBC News found that 58% of those asked agreed with the statement that Mondale had "promised too many things to special interest groups," and of those who agreed with that statement, 54% voted for Hart and 9% for Mondale.[23] In fact, Hart outpolled Mondale among union households in New Hampshire by a margin of 43 to 38 percentage points.[24]

Current election polls suggest that whatever else the backing of organized labor has brought Walter Mondale, it has not yet brought him overwhelming support from membership. A survey completed by Richard Wirthlin, the President's pollster, in June of 1984 found the President preferred by 52% of blue-collar voters, with 38% supporting Mondale; when the sample focused on union members, Mondale was preferred by a margin of 50% to 40%.[25] A poll of voters in Michigan—one of the most heavily unionized states—published in the *New York Times* the same month found Ronald Reagan preferred by 50% of the union members surveyed, Walter Mondale by 49%. This was a narrower lead for the President than he had in the survey as a whole—where 55% backed him, compared to 39% for Walter Mondale.[26] Even when facing a candidate without the unpopularity of Jimmy Carter, and after the most intensive involvement on behalf of a presidential candidate by organized labor *ever*, Ronald Reagan continues to draw substantial voters from rank and file union members.

When we asked our sample to choose between Ronald Reagan and Walter Mondale, 50.2% chose Mondale and 33.2% chose Reagan. There was once again a significant gap between union activists and non-activists; Mondale's margin among activists was 28.2 percentage points, and among non-activists it was only 12.1 percentage points. (See Table 34)

Table 34.

"If this year's 1984 election for President were held today and you had to make a choice, for which of the following candidates would you probably vote—(1) Ronald Reagan, the Republican, or (2) Walter Mondale, the Democrat?"

	Reagan	Undecided	Mondale
Union Activists	25.7	20.4	53.9
Non-Activists	36.5	14.9	48.6

When we broke the sample down into classes of voters, we found Mondale's greatest margin of victory—20.8 percentage points—among upper white-collar workers, and the narrowest margin—5 percentage points—among lower blue-collar workers. (See Table 35)

Table 35. Reagan/Mondale

	Reagan	Undecided	Mondale
Upper White-Collar	29.6	20.0	50.4
Lower White-Collar	34.3	14.9	50.7
Upper Blue-Collar	35.6	11.0	53.4
Lower Blue-Collar	37.6	19.8	42.6

Mondale's margin among white Protestants and white Catholics was significantly narrower than that in the sample as a whole, but his margin among other white ethnic groups and among blacks was significantly wider. (See Table 36)

Table 36. Reagan/Mondale

	Reagan	Undecided	Mondale
White Catholic	34.6	20.5	44.9
White Protestant	39.7	17.3	43.0
White Other	35.3	14.7	50.0
Black	9.5	11.1	79.4

We then paired the President with Senator Gary Hart. In many ways, the Hart and Mondale campaigns sought and won different sets of voters. Mondale, with his roots in the Democratic-Farmer-Labor Party of Minnesota and a lifetime of visiting union halls, pitched his campaign to a traditional Roosevelt working-class constituency. Gary Hart, a Yale-educated Westerner, pitched his ideas to young, upwardly mobile professionals. The tension was perhaps best illustrated by a sign held up by a Mondale supporter at one of Hart's rallies: "We can't all be computer programmers."

In some states, like New Hampshire, Hart did quite well with union voters. In other states, like Pennsylvania, the union vote went to Mondale. In our survey, there was virtually the same aggregate support for Hart against Reagan as there was for Mondale against Reagan. Hart was chosen by 49.6% of the respondents, and Reagan by 34.6%. The gap between the activists and non-activists was stronger here; Hart won among the activists by a margin of 31.6 percentage points, and among the non-activists by only 7.8 percentage points. (See Table 37)

Table 37. Reagan/Hart

	Reagan	Undecided	Hart
Union Activists	27.0	14.5	58.6
Non-Activists	37.9	16.4	45.7

One interesting note, in light of the much-discussed "gender gap": we found that while Ronald Reagan drew significantly better among men than he did among women, Mondale and Hart each drew virtually the same proportion among women as they did among men. The flip side of the gap between male and female support for Reagan was found not in support for the opponent, but in the undecided column, where the figure for women was higher than that for men. (See Table 38)

Table 38. Reagan/Mondale

	Reagan	Undecided	Mondale
Male	36.0	13.7	50.3
Female	28.5	21.5	50.0

We asked those surveyed their views about Jesse Jackson. His name identification was high—95.5% correctly identified him. He was viewed favorably by 41.7%, unfavorably by 31.9%, and 21.9% had no opinion. When we broke our sample down, we found these figures masked some of the greatest divergences among sub-groups of any of the questions we asked.

The margin in the total sample between favorable and unfavorable opinion was 9.8 percentage points. We once again found that breaking the sample into union activists and non-activists revealed deep division. Among non-activists, the favorable/unfavorable gap was 4 points; among activists, it was 23. (See Table 39)

Table 39. Jesse Jackson

(These numbers do not add up to 100, because we eliminated those who could not identify Jackson)

	Favorable	Unfavorable	No Opinion
Union Activists	50.3	27.3	17.4
Non-Activists	37.9	33.9	23.9

Another dramatic disparity was that between different unions. The gap between favorable and unfavorable ratings among AFL-CIO members was 0.4 percentage points; for Teamsters, 2.6 percentage points; for government employees, 20 percentage points; and for educators 35.5 percentage points. (See Table 40)

Table 40. Jesse Jackson

	Favorable	Unfavorable	No Opinion
AFL-CIO	37.0	36.6	22.0
Teamsters	34.2	31.6	25.0
Education/Schools	57.2	21.7	18.1
Government Related	50.0	30.0	20.0

Consistent with these figures, Jackson's greatest favorable/unfavorable ratio came from the upper white-collar and best educated union members, somewhat paradoxical when put in the context of a campaign directed at the "locked out," the "dispossessed," and the "boats stuck at the bottom." The gap between favorable and unfavorable among white collar workers was 25.3 points, but only 2.8 points among lower blue-collar workers. Among those who had done post graduate work (a category in which teachers, of course, were disproportionately represented) the gap was 44.1 points while among those without a high school diploma, the *unfavorable* rating was actually 4.1 points higher than the favorable rating. (See Table 41)

Table 41. Jesse Jackson

	Favorable	Unfavorable	No Opinion
Upper White-Collar	51.1	25.8	19.7
Lower White-Collar	43.7	31.1	21.5
Upper Blue-Collar	36.8	36.8	21.8
Lower Blue-Collar	36.3	33.5	23.1
Less Than High School	33.0	37.1	22.7
High School Graduate	34.2	36.2	23.6
Some College	40.0	33.5	23.7
College Graduate	54.0	22.6	20.2
Post Graduate Work	63.8	19.7	14.2

In presenting our respondents with choices for the 1984 presidential election, we split our sample in two. Half were asked the question discussed earlier, in which Reagan and Mondale were put head to head.

The others were asked an identically worded question that presented a choice between a ticket of Ronald Reagan and George Bush and a ticket of Walter Mondale and Jesse Jackson. We did this not because Jackson was ever a likely vice-presidential pick, but because it focused attention on how people reacted to Jackson as a political candidate instead of whether they generally felt favorably or unfavorably disposed towards him. With Jackson's presence on the Mondale ticket, what had been a lead of 17 percentage points narrowed to 6.2. (See Table 42)

Table 42. Reagan-Bush vs. Mondale-Jackson

	Percentage Response
Reagan-Bush	39.0
Undecided	11.6
Mondale-Jackson	45.2

Adding Jackson led to a Reagan victory among white Catholics and white Protestants, but led to a wider margin of victory for Mondale among other white ethnic groups and among blacks. (See Table 43)

Table 43. Reagan-Bush vs. Mondale-Jackson

	Reagan-Bush	Mondale-Jackson	Undecided
White Catholic	43.7	35.7	20.6
White Protestant	48.5	37.2	14.3
White Other	27.7	55.4	16.9
Black	2.1	91.7	6.3

The addition of Jackson to the ticket actually widened the already substantial gap between activists and non-activists. With Jackson on the Mondale ticket, Ronald Reagan outpolled Walter Mondale among non-activists by 4.6 percentage points, while Mondale outpolled Reagan among activists by 31 percentage points. (See Table 44)

Table 44. Reagan-Bush vs. Mondale-Jackson

	Reagan-Bush	Mondale-Jackson	Undecided
Union Activists	27.6	58.6	13.8
Non-Activists	44.0	39.4	16.7

Conclusions

Union voters have generally been considered—appropriately so—part of the bedrock constituency of the Democratic Party. Therefore, if a Republican can attract even a substantial *minority* of union votes, he can generally win an election. Our survey did not discover that a majority of union members support Ronald Reagan. However, if Ronald Reagan during the course of his campaign can build somewhat on the union support found in this poll—as he did in 1980—while retaining traditional Republican constituencies, he is unlikely to be defeated.

Our survey suggests, however, that rank and file support for the President is largely *personal*—he is perceived as a strong and trustworthy leader, and from that flows much of his support. Ronald Reagan has attracted significant working class votes, but he has not brought about any sort of permanent realignment. What Ronald Reagan has demonstrated is simply that enough of the working class is and will continue to be up for grabs to make their support worth the effort of conservatives and Republicans. It is a vote which will go by default to the Democrats, but one which Republicans with the right image and philosophy can successfully contest, since "success" for Republicans in an election may only require a *piece* of the union vote.

Chapter 3
Attitudes Towards Unions

We probed the respondents' attitudes toward their unions and unions generally, examining the degree to which the members do or do not identify with the political positions taken by organized labor. The results were unambiguous. The rank and file perceive union political activity as unrepresentativeness of their views, and this perception becomes particularly strong when the members are asked to focus on *national* union leadership.

We asked those surveyed whether they agreed or disagreed with the following statement:

> "The national leadership of my union pretty well represents my own personal views on political and social issues."

Fully 57.5% disagreed with that statement, 40% disagreeing strongly. (See Table 45)

Table 45. "Pretty Well Represents My Views"

	Percentage Response
Agree Strongly	16.9
Agree	17.5
Unsure	7.1
Disagree	17.5
Disagree Strongly	40.0
Don't Know/No Answer	1.0

In none of the four categories of unions we surveyed—AFL-CIO, Teamsters, Education/Schools or Government Related—did those who agreed with the statement outnumber those who disagreed. The educators expressed the least disagreement—49.4% disagreed while 42.8% agreed (the rest were unsure)—and the Teamsters registered the most disagreement—68.4% feeling unrepresented. Once again, we found demonstrably different attitudes between the activists and the non-activists, although, remarkably, even among the activists there was more disagreement with the statement than agreement. Fully 49.0% of the activists disagreed with the statement (with 44.1% agreeing), and 61.2% of the non-activists agreed, with 30.2% disagreeing. (See Table 46)

Table 46. "Pretty Well Represents My Views"

	Agree Strongly	Agree	Unsure	Disagree	Disagree Strongly	Don't Know No Answer
Union Activists	23.4	20.7	6.6	15.8	33.2	0.3
Non-Activists	14.1	16.1	7.3	18.2	43.0	1.3

Those who said they voted "mostly Democratic" *agreed* with the statement by a margin of 49.9% to 42.6%; those who voted "slightly Democratic," "Republican," or for "the man" all registered greater disagreement than they did agreement. (See Table 47)

Table 47. "Pretty Well Represents My Views"

	Agree Strongly	Agree	Unsure	Disagree	Disagree Strongly	Don't Know No Answer
Republican	6.7	8.2	4.1	19.1	61.3	0.5
The Man	9.4	13.3	11.4	17.6	47.1	1.2
Slightly Democratic	15.1	23.0	5.9	20.4	34.9	0.7
Mostly Democratic	27.3	22.6	6.3	15.5	27.1	1.3

In addition, we found strong differences among different age groups. While 50.9% of union members ages 45 and older disagreed with the statement, fully 62.1% of union members ages 18-44 felt unrepresented.

Disagreement may take many forms. The next problem was to identify the *direction* of disagreement. Did members feel the national leadership of their union was too liberal, or too conservative, or was the difference not clearly ideological? We asked a series of questions to determine the nature of the disagreement.

We began by asking the respondents their ideology:

"When thinking about politics and government, do you consider yourself to be (1) very conservative, (2) somewhat conservative, (3) somewhat liberal, or (4) very liberal?"

(We did not include "moderate," because "moderate" is simply too attractive a choice, and we wanted those surveyed to take some step in defining themselves. If they volunteered "moderate" as an answer, we recorded it.) A majority—52.9%—defined themselves as conservative; 40% defined themselves as liberal. (See Table 48)

Table 48. Personal Ideology

	Percentage Response
Very Conservative	11.4
Somewhat Conservative	41.5
Moderate	5.4
Somewhat Liberal	33.0
Very Liberal	7.0
Don't Know/No Answer	1.7

Most of the different unions' members expressed ideological preferences in rough proportion to the total sample, although government employees were significantly more liberal, and in fact this was the only category of union members where liberals outnumbered conservative (55.0% to 42.5%). The better educated, high-status employees tended to be more liberal. Lower white-collar workers, and upper and lower blue-collar workers, were more likely to describe themselves as conservative than liberal, while upper white-collar workers described themselves as liberal more often than they did conservative. (See Table 49)

Table 49. Personal Ideology

	Very Cons.	Somewhat Cons.	Moderate	Somewhat Lib.	Very Lib.
Upper White-Collar	6.1	37.9	6.4	42.8	6.8
Lower White-Collar	8.9	40.7	8.9	31.1	10.4
Upper Blue-Collar	11.2	45.4	5.2	30.7	7.5
Lower Blue-Collar	14.3	41.2	8.2	30.2	6.0
Less than High School	19.6	41.2	9.3	23.7	6.2
High School Graduate	12.7	42.4	7.4	31.5	6.0
Some College	10.6	42.9	6.9	34.7	4.9
College Graduate	7.3	36.3	8.9	34.7	12.9
Post Graduate Work	6.3	40.9	3.1	40.9	8.7

We then asked those surveyed to characterize the local leadership of their union in ideological terms:

> "Which best describes the local leadership of your union at the local level— (1) very conservative, (2) somewhat conservative, (3) somewhat liberal, or (4) very liberal?

More of our respondents labeled their local leadership conservative than liberal, but the gap between the two figures was narrower than the gap between those who considered *themselves* conservatives and those who considered *themselves* liberal. (See Table 50)

Table 50. Ideology of Local Leadership

	Percentage Response
Very Conservative	13.1
Somewhat Conservative	32.2
Moderate	3.0
Somewhat Liberal	31.3
Very Liberal	12.2
Don't Know/No Answer	8.2

Clearly, there was feeling among some members that their local leadership was more liberal than they themselves were.

We next moved up a level, and asked the respondents to characterize the ideology of the national leadership of their union:

> "Which of these best describes the national leadership of your union—(1) very conservative, (2) somewhat conservative, (3) somewhat liberal, or (4) very liberal?"

At this level, those who perceived the leadership to be liberal outnumbered those who saw the leadership as conservative, 48.0% to 39.8%. (See Table 51)

Table 51. Ideology of National Leadership

	Percentage Response
Very Conservative	10.9
Somewhat Conservative	28.9
Moderate	3.2
Somewhat Liberal	33.1
Very Liberal	14.9
Don't Know/No Answer	9.0

Educators were most likely to label their national leadership liberal—57.3% did so. AFL-CIO members and government employees were also more likely than not to label their leadership as liberal. The only exception to this pattern were the Teamsters, and they by the closest of margins. While 43.4% of the Teamsters labeled their national leadership as somewhat or very liberal, 44.7% labeled the national leadership as somewhat or very conservative.

The final step was to ask those surveyed about unions generally:

"And which of these best describes the leaders of unions and organized labor in this country—(1) very conservative, (2) somewhat conservative, (3) somewhat liberal, or (4) very liberal?"

This completed the trend. Fully 53.0% of the respondents labeled the national leadership of organized labor as liberal, and only 33.1% labeled the national leadership conservative. (See Table 52)

Table 52. Ideology of Unions Generally

	Percentage Response
Very Conservative	8.4
Somewhat Conservative	24.7
Moderate	4.1
Somewhat Liberal	35.7
Very Liberal	17.3
Don't Know/No Answer	9.8

Thus, as the leadership on which the question is focused is distanced further and further from the individual union member, that member becomes less and less likely to see himself as politically represented. The perception that leadership was liberal—and more liberal than the members perceived themselves to be—was strengthened as the questions moved from local to national unions, and from the members' own unions to national unions in general.

The feeling of distance from national leadership is strong, but it is characterized more by indifference than resentment. We asked a name identification question about Lane Kirkland, identical in form to that asked earlier about Jesse Jackson. Whereas in Jackson's case, 1.2% had never heard of him, 3.0% had heard of him but could not identify him, and 95.5% knew who he was, 60.1% of our sample had *never heard of* Lane Kirkland, and 21.4% had heard of him but could not identify him. Of the 18.5% remaining that knew who he was, 7.2% had no opinion, favorable or unfavorable, about the President of the AFL-CIO. (See Table 53)

Table 53. Lane Kirkland

	Percentage Response
Never Heard of	60.1
Heard of Only	21.4
Know/Favorable	8.5
Know/Unfavorable	2.8
Know/No Opinion	7.2

In fact, members of the AFL-CIO were only slightly more familiar with the name than the others in our sample; 57.5% of AFL-CIO members surveyed had never heard of Lane Kirkland, and 20.3% had heard of the name but were unable to identify him.

These are striking numbers. Lane Kirkland is the President of the AFL-CIO, the undisputedly dominant labor leader in the country. Yet the vast majority of union members have no idea who he is. This suggests a number of things.

First, it suggests a genuine indifference on the part of the rank and file to the national leadership and its activities. Any union member even mildly interested in following the national labor movement would have run into the name of Lane Kirkland early on. Those who cannot identify him are clearly completely disinterested.

Second, it suggests a distance between leadership and membership that renders leadership unaccountable to those for whom it claims to speak. Those who cannot identify Lane Kirkland are unlikely to have any clear idea of what positions he takes or candidates he endorses, and hence will not react or protest when that representation is misguided.

Third, it indicates an acquiescence on the part of the rank and file. Apathy of this magnitude might normally suggest that membership reposes confidence and trust in its leadership, but that is belied by the answers to our other questions. Yet despite the large number of members who feel themselves unrepresented, few think it important enough to work for change.

Finally, despite the obvious responsibility borne by the rank and file, these numbers suggest that Lane Kirkland and the national leadership of organized labor have themselves made no serious effort to become known to their constituents. Apathy frees them from a great many headaches. The *Washington Post* reports:

> "Kirkland does not view the rank and file as his primary constituency, says one colleague. He is old school in that he sees the international union presidents who make up the AFL-CIO general board, themselves an increasingly sophisticated bunch, as his real constituency. Ask them, they say he's doing just fine. He's 'collegial'. They trust him."[1]

This elitism is only possible in the context of widespread membership disinterest, and the freedom of action it grants leadership makes it unlikely that this same leadership will seek to truly expand participation and decisionmaking down to the rank and file.

In fact, most of our respondents did not even believe political activity ought be a high priority of their local labor union. We asked the following question:

"I'm going to read several different activities that your local union leaders could be involved in. For each one, please tell me if it should be a top priority of your local union leaders, an important priority, or a low priority for your local union leaders:

- Negotiating contracts for your union
- Handling general grievances lodged by your union members.
- Endorsing candidates for political office."

Negotiating contracts was labeled a "top priority" by 79.5%, 15.2% labeling it an important priority, and 3.1% a "low priority." Grievances were labeled a top priority by 65.7%, an important priority by 28.0%, and a low priority by 5.0%. In contrast, endorsing candidates was held a top priority by 10.5%, an important priority by 24.2%, and a low priority by 61.6%. Those who voted "mostly Democratic" were significantly more likely to label political endorsements a top or important priority. (See Table 54)

Table 54. Endorsing Candidates

	Top Prior.	Imp. Prior.	Low Prior.	Unsure
Republican	3.6	16.0	78.9	1.5
The Man	6.3	19.2	69.8	4.7
Slightly Democratic	6.6	28.3	64.5	0.7
Mostly Democratic	18.8	29.8	46.9	4.5

These results were certainly not surprising in any way, but they suggest an explanation of why union members elect leaders they often do not believe will share their political views, and of why there is such apathy regarding national leadership. Unions are important to their members largely because of the job-related services they provide. Members likely choose and judge union officers primarily on the basis of their success in bringing members a good wage, decent working conditions, and job security, and these are responsibilities predominantly of local leadership. Lane Kirkland does not negotiate contracts. Because the political views of leadership are somewhat incidental to what members regard as the function of their trade unions, there is no reason to expect the political views of membership to be clearly reflected by leadership, either now or in the future. The incentives that exist in most representative bodies for the representatives to fairly represent the represented are absent from the decisionmaking that attends labor involvement in politics. Negotiating a weak contract may well get union leadership replaced; endorsing the "wrong" candidate is unlikely to matter.

In addition to believing that political activity ought to be a low priority, most of those surveyed believed that union leadership devotes excessive attention to politics. We asked our sample to agree or disagree with the following statement:

> "Unions in this country spend too much time on politics and political issues, and not enough time on fighting for better wages and working conditions."

That statement was endorsed by 51.0% of our sample, with 37.4% disagreeing. (See Table 55)

Table 55. Unions Spend Too Much Time on Politics

	Percentage Response
Agree Strongly	39.8
Agree	11.2
Unsure	10.2
Disagree	14.4
Disagree Strongly	23.0
Don't Know/No Answer	1.4

While union activists tended to *disagree* with this statement by a margin of 50.0% to 43.4%, non-activists *agreed* with the statement by a margin of 54.3% to 31.9%. Educators agreed with the statement by the smallest margin—44.2% to 43.0%—while Teamsters agreed by the widest margin—65.0% to 22.5%.

We next asked those surveyed to register their agreement or disagreement with the following strongly-worded statement:

> "The national leadership of my union is more interested in their own personal power and glory than the concerns of the members of the union."

While a bare majority of the respondents—52.6%—disagreed with that statement, a substantial minority—37.6%—agreed. (See Table 56)

Table 56. Leadership Interested in Personal Power

	Percentage Response
Agree Strongly	26.4
Agree	11.2
Unsure	9.2
Disagree	18.2
Disagree Strongly	34.4
Don't Know/No Answer	0.6

By a more than 2-to-1 margin (63.9% to 30.6%), Teamsters agreed with the statement, undoubtedly reflecting widespread reports of corruption within that union's leadership. While only 29.6% of the activists in our survey agreed with the statement, 41.1% of the non-activists indicated their agreement.

The general conclusions to be drawn from these data seem clear. Union members by and large do not view their national unions as particularly representative bodies, nor do they view their unions as organizations that ought to be deeply involved in politics. Membership perceives itself as generally to the ideological right of leadership. Thus, when we asked those surveyed to answer the following question:

> "Generally speaking, and trying to be as honest as you can, are you generally more likely to vote for a candidate your union endorses, less likely to vote for that candidate, or does the fact that your union endorses a candidate make no difference in how you vote?"

the overwhelming majority—86.2% —said the union endorsement made no difference. (Even among union activists, 83.6% indicated that it made "no difference".)

It is therefore fair to say not only that union endorsements do not necessarily reflect the views of the rank and file, but also that the existence of an endorsement is unlikely to bring many of their votes along. This is not to deny that organized labor backing can be instrumental in winning elections; the resources of these organizations are quite substantial. But it seems clear that the political activists operate on a plane far removed from the concerns, ideas and interests of the rank and file.

Chapter 4
Subsamples

As this monograph has proceeded from question to question, we have frequently noted the ways in which various groups within our total sample have differed in their responses. In this chapter, we will examine some of these subsamples in greater detail, and make some generalizations about their responses across categories of questions.

Activists and Non-Activists

Our survey was in part an attempt to ascertain what tensions exist between the positions taken by union leadership and the views of the rank and file. Many of the rank and file, however, are integrated to some extent within the leadership as well. In order to determine whether the views of those union members differed significantly from the views of the sample as a whole, we developed a category—"union activist"—which consisted of those people who answered affirmatively to the following question:

> "Some union members have the time and inclination to be active in their union affairs, while others don't. How about you? Do you now or have you in the past held union offices or served on union committees, or not?"

Union activists comprised 30.4% of our total sample. 61.2% of them were between the ages of 18 and 44. 51.0% of them had a family income of $30,000 or more, as opposed to only 40.4% of the non-activists. A disproportionate number—24.3%—belonged to an education union, with the largest bloc—54.9%—members of the AFL-CIO. Their ethnic and racial background pretty closely mirrored that of the sample as a whole, but there was a slightly higher percentage of activists who were men—66.8%—than there were of men in our total sample—63.2%.

While there were a few questions—such as the one on defense spending—over which the differences were small, there were many more in which the differences were quite substantial. For example, by a margin of 15.3 percentage points, a higher percentage of non-activists approved of Ronald Reagan's job performance; by a margin of 8 percentage points, non-activists described their voting behavior as Republican more often than did activists; a Mondale-Jackson ticket defeated Reagan-Bush 58.6% to 27.6% among activists, but *lost* 44.0% to 39.4% among non-activists.

Table 57. Activists vs. Non-Activists

	Union Activists	Non-Activists
Defense Spending		
Increase	30.3	32.0
Unsure	18.1	20.0
Decrease	51.6	48.0
Budget Policy: Dislike		
Raise Federal Income Taxes	29.7	34.4
Cut Federal Programs and Services	30.6	28.0
Continue to Borrow Money	35.6	34.2
Don't Know/No Answer	4.1	3.5
Tuition Tax Credits		
Favor	41.8	45.8
Unsure	5.6	6.9
Oppose	52.6	47.3
Competency Tests		
Favor	78.1	84.7
Unsure	2.3	3.7
Oppose	19.6	11.6
Ronald Reagan		
Approve Strongly	15.5	24.9
Approve	14.5	20.4
Undecided	11.8	9.6
Disapprove	10.9	11.5
Disapprove Strongly	46.1	33.0
Don't Know/No Answer	1.3	0.6
Lane Kirkland		
Never Heard Of	50.0	64.5
Heard of Only	24.3	20.1
Know/Favorable	14.8	5.7
Know/Unfavorable	2.6	2.9
Know/No Opinion	8.2	6.8
Jesse Jackson		
Never Heard Of	1.6	1.4
Heard of Only	3.3	2.9
Know/Favorable	50.3	37.9
Know/Unfavorable	27.3	33.9
Know/No Opinion	17.4	23.9
Comparable Worth: First Question		
Favor	90.8	86.8
Unsure	2.6	3.3
Oppose	6.6	9.9

	Union Activists	Non-Activists
Comparable Worth: Follow-up		
(asked of those who favored)		
Still Favor (as a percentage of *total* sample)	57.2	49.6
Now Oppose (as a percentage of *total* sample)	33.6	37.2
Endorsing Candidates		
Top Priority	14.1	9.3
Important Priority	26.3	23.3
Low Priority	55.3	64.4
Unsure	4.3	3.0
Voting Behavior		
Republican	13.8	21.8
The Man	19.7	28.0
Slightly Democratic	16.4	14.7
Mostly Democratic	50.0	35.5
Reagan vs. Mondale		
Reagan	25.7	36.5
Undecided	20.4	14.9
Mondale	53.9	48.6
Reagan-Bush vs. Mondale-Jackson		
Reagan-Bush	27.6	44.0
Undecided	13.8	16.7
Mondale-Jackson	58.6	39.4
Effect of Union Endorsement on Your Vote		
More Likely to Support Candidate	12.8	7.5
Less Likely to Support Candidate	3.6	4.2
No Difference	83.6	88.4
National Leadership Represents My Views		
Agree	44.1	30.2
Unsure	6.9	8.6
Disagree	49.0	61.2
National Leadership Interested in Personal Power		
Agree	29.6	41.1
Unsure	13.2	8.3
Disagree	57.2	50.6
Unions Spend Too Much Time on Politics		
Agree	43.4	54.3
Unsure	6.6	13.8
Disagree	50.0	31.9

Activists were much more likely to take positions generally characterized as "liberal," and to support left-of-center political candidates. Perhaps the general political orientation of organized labor naturally encourages those with similar views to think of the organizations as ones in which they would be comfortable exercising leadership, and thus attracts people of like views into the leadership structure. Or perhaps serving as a union official has its own influence, and serves to help shape an ideology through the associations and experiences it provides. Whatever the cause, the results are unambiguous.

When we asked our respondents to agree or disagree with a variety of statements about unions and union political activity, it was not surprising to find union activists demonstrating greater feelings of support and loyalty to their unions than non-activists. What was surprising was the degree to which *even the activists* would agree with statements critical of labor leadership. Thus, while union activists did not disagree with the statement that the national leadership "pretty well represents my own personal views on political and social issues" by the 2-to-1 margin that non-activists did, they nevertheless disagreed more than they agreed, with fully 49.0% feeling unrepresented. It was perhaps predictable that a higher percentage of activists than non-activists would disagree with the statement that "the national leadership of my union is more interested in their own personal power and glory than the concerns of the members of the union," but it was *not* predictable that as strong a statement as that would find 42.8% of the activists either agreeing or unsure. And while it is interesting that the statement "unions in this country spend too much time on politics and political issues and not enough time fighting for better wages and working conditions" found more agreement than disagreement among non-activists, and more disagreement than agreement among activists, it is even more interesting that only 50.0% of the activists said they disagreed.

Different Unions

Union membership in our sample broke down along the following lines:

AFL-CIO	546
Teamsters	76
Education/	
Schools	166
Government	80
Other	77
No Answer	55
	1000

Our union activists were disproportionately members of education unions—44.6% of those in education unions were activists, as compared with 30.6% of the AFL-CIO members, 22.5% of the government employees, and 19.7% of the Teamsters. Teamsters constituted our youngest subsample—40.8% were under 35—while educators and government employees were our oldest—with 70.5% and 71.4%, respectively, 35 or older. Catholics were unusually well represented among government employees—42.5% of whom were Catholics—while educators were predominantly (48.2%) Protestant. Educators were mostly women, while AFL-CIO members and Teamsters were disproportionately male. Government employees were mostly men, but by a narrower margin than the sample as a whole:

	Male	Female
AFL-CIO	71.8	28.2
Teamsters	81.6	18.4
Education/Schools	29.5	70.5
Government Related	57.5	42.5

AFL-CIO members and Teamsters were the ones in our sample who had suffered the most unemployment; 24.7% of our AFL-CIO members, and 27.6% of our Teamsters, had been unemployed for some time in the past year. Only 5.4% of the educators and 5.1% of the government employees made that claim. The educators were the wealthiest—51.2% have a family income of $30,000 a year or more—with the AFL-CIO members the least well off—54.8% with a family income less than $30,000 a year. Educators, of course were also the best educated; 57.2% of them had done some post-graduate work, while a plurality of government employees—40.0%—had attended some college but not received a diploma, and 48.0% and 52.6% of the AFL-CIO members and Teamsters, respectively, had graduated from high school and not gone further.

Issues that had their greatest impact on a particular profession or class of profession generally provoked unique responses within those professions. Thus, educators reacted strongly to the idea of tuition tax credits and competency tests, and Teamsters and AFL-CIO members were supportive of domestic content laws by much higher percentages than educators and government employees.

Ideological patterns were somewhat mixed. Educators, Teamsters and AFL-CIO members were all more likely to characterize themselves as conservative than liberal; government employees were the only category in which self-described liberals outnumbered self-described conservatives.

 SOLIDARITY AND DISSENT

Table 58. Attitudes By Union

	AFL-CIO	Team-sters	Education/ Schools	Gov't Related
Defense Spending				
Increase	33.7	43.4	24.1	21.3
Unsure	19.0	15.8	17.5	27.5
Decrease	47.3	40.8	58.4	51.3
Tuition Tax Credit				
Favor	44.7	48.7	36.1	48.8
Unsure	7.5	7.9	4.2	5.0
Oppose	47.8	43.4	59.6	46.3
Affirmative Action—First Question				
Favor	70.0	75.0	75.9	71.3
Unsure	7.5	5.3	7.2	8.8
Oppose	22.5	19.7	16.9	20.0
Affirmative action: Follow-up (Special Treatment) **(asked of those who said they favored)**				
Still Favor (as a percentage of *total* sample)	22.2	35.5	31.3	25.0
Now Oppose (as a percentage of *total* sample)	47.8	39.5	44.6	46.3
Competency Tests				
Favor	91.0	83.0	54.7	92.1
Unsure	1.9	6.4	3.1	3.2
Oppose	7.1	10.6	42.2	4.8
Domestic Content: First Question				
Favor	78.9	90.8	60.8	61.3
Unsure	7.1	0.0	9.6	12.5
Oppose	13.9	9.2	29.5	26.3
Domestic Content: Follow-up **(asked of those who said they favored)**				
Still Favor (as a percentage of *total* sample)	65.9	75.0	51.8	52.5
Now Oppose (as a percentage of *total* sample)	13.0	15.8	9.0	8.8
Ronald Reagan				
Approve Strongly	21.2	36.8	18.7	22.5
Approve	17.0	21.1	27.7	12.5
Unsure	11.2	7.9	9.6	8.8
Disapprove	11.4	7.9	9.6	15.0
Disapprove Strongly	38.6	26.3	32.5	40.0
Don't Know/No Answer	0.5	0.0	1.8	1.3
Jesse Jackson				
Never Heard Of	1.5	2.6	1.2	0.0
Heard of Only	2.9	6.6	1.8	0.0
Know/Favorable	37.0	34.2	57.2	50.0
Know/Unfavorable	36.6	31.6	21.7	30.0
Know/No Opinion	22.0	25.0	18.1	20.0

	AFL-CIO	Team-sters	Education/ Schools	Gov't Related
Comparable Worth: First Question				
Favor	86.4	90.8	92.8	88.8
Unsure	2.6	1.3	2.4	7.5
Oppose	11.0	7.9	4.8	3.8
Comparable Worth: Follow-up **(asked of those who favor)**				
Still Favor (as a percentage of *total* sample)	47.6	52.6	65.1	57.5
Now Oppose (as a percentage of *total* sample)	38.8	38.2	27.7	31.3
Personal Ideology				
Very Conservative	12.1	13.2	9.6	2.5
Somewhat Conservative	42.1	39.5	42.8	40.0
Moderate	8.2	6.6	6.0	2.5
Somewhat Liberal	31.3	34.2	33.1	45.0
Very Liberal	6.2	6.6	8.4	10.0
Ideology of National Leadership of Your Union				
Very Conervative	12.6	18.4	4.8	6.3
Somewhat Conservative	28.2	26.3	28.3	26.3
Moderate	13.0	11.8	9.6	16.3
Somewhat Liberal	30.4	27.6	44.0	40.0
Very Liberal	15.8	15.8	13.3	11.3
Voting Behavior				
Republican	16.8	27.6	25.3	16.3
The Man	26.0	34.2	16.3	32.5
Slightly Democratic	15.4	7.9	21.7	13.8
Mostly Democratic	41.8	30.3	36.7	37.5
Reagan vs. Mondale				
Reagan	32.6	50.0	37.5	27.5
Undecided	13.1	16.7	21.3	15.0
Mondale	54.3	33.3	41.3	57.5
National Leadership of My Union Represents My Views				
Agree	34.4	25.0	42.8	28.8
Unsure	7.1	6.6	7.8	11.3
Disagree	58.4	68.4	49.4	60.0
National Leadership of My Union Interested in Personal Power				
Agree	40.8	63.9	21.3	25.0
Unsure	11.2	5.6	6.3	7.5
Disagree	47.9	30.6	72.5	67.5
Unions Spend Too Much Time on Politics				
Agree	49.8	65.0	44.2	52.5
Unsure	11.1	12.5	12.8	10.0
Disagree	39.1	22.5	43.0	37.5

Nevertheless, what our respondents meant when they called themselves conservatives often differed.

Teamsters seemed to most closely fit the conservative label. This was the only category of respondents in which those favoring increases in defense spending outnumbered those favoring decreases. Along with government employees, they were the most supportive of tuition tax credits. They were the most Republican, the most approving of Ronald Reagan, and most likely to choose Reagan over Mondale. Along with the AFL-CIO members, they were the most likely to have an unfavorable opinion of Jesse Jackson. The one quirk in this pattern was their position on affirmative action: they were the category in our sample most likely to *favor* special treatment. Perhaps most predictable: they indicated the greatest dislike and distrust of their union leadership, not surprising given the scandals constantly plaguing the Teamsters.

The members of the AFL-CIO gave a somewhat paradoxical response. They generally defined themselves as conservatives, and their issue positions were often more conservative than the sample as a whole. Their support for defense spending was topped only by the Teamsters; they were the most opposed to affirmative action when defined in terms of special treatment; along with the Teamsters, they were the least supportive of comparable worth and most unfavorably disposed towards Jesse Jackson. Yet their approval rating for Ronald Reagan was the lowest, and, with the exception of the government employees, they gave the greatest support to Walter Mondale. They demonstrated perhaps the largest discrepency between their philosophy and their election choices, suggesting that they are a group in which conservatives could make significant inroads.

The educators presented the opposite paradox. They also tended to describe themselves as conservatives. However, they were the most opposed to defense spending, the most supportive, next to the Teamsters, of special treatment for minorities, the most favorable to Jesse Jackson and the most supportive of comparable worth. They nevertheless were second only to the Teamsters in their support for Ronald Reagan and the Republican Party. Their positions on the issues, therefore, suggest that they are a group from which liberal candidates should and can be drawing more support than they currently are, at least in the upcoming presidential contest. Unlike AFL-CIO members, they do not seem to be a group in any way predisposed to accept politically conservative ideologies.

Government employees were the only group with a majority of self-described liberals, and their responses bore out the characterization. Next to teachers, they were the most in favor of defense cuts; they were most supportive of comparable worth, very favorable to Jesse Jackson, and most opposed to Ronald Reagan. Perhaps the only quirk in their figures was their plurality support for tuition tax credits.

Social Status

There are several categories subsumed here: family income, job status and educational background. For the most part, upper white-collar workers were the highest paid and best educated, and salary and educational background diminished as our sample moved from upper white-collar to lower white-collar and upper blue-collar to lower blue-collar. Hence, for the purpose of clarity, we limit ourselves here to job status, recognizing that it serves as a partial proxy for these other indices as well.

Our sample broke down as follows:

Upper White-Collar	264
Lower White-Collar	135
Upper Blue-Collar	348
Lower Blue-Collar	182
All Others	71
	1000

51.1% of the upper white-collar workers were educators, 25.0% belonged to the AFL-CIO, and 13.3% were government employees. 57.8% of the lower white-collar workers were AFL-CIO members, with 14.8% in government and 11.9% in the schools. The upper blue-collar workers were overwhelmingly (74.1%) AFL-CIO, with most of the remainder (12.1%) Teamsters, and the lower blue-collar workers were divided mostly between the AFL-CIO (55.5%) and unions which did not fit into our four major categories (21.4%).

Some issues were of particular interest to one segment or another. Thus, blue-collar workers were predictably more supportive of domestic content laws and more opposed to amnesty for illegal immigrants, while white-collar workers were more strongly supportive of comparable worth.

In many others areas, the more upper-scale voters were frequently the more liberal. Thus, upper white-collar workers were the most supportive of defense cuts, the most opposed to cutting federal programs and services, the least opposed to raising income taxes, the most disapproving of Ronald Reagan, the most favorably disposed toward Jesse Jackson, the most supportive of comparable worth, and the most likely to describe themselves as liberals. In some instances—such as defense spending and approval ratings for the President—the upper white-collar numbers were most similar to the lower blue-collar numbers, with the more conservative positions taken by the ones in the middle—the lower white-collar workers and the upper blue-collar workers. In other instances, such as budget policy, the trend was steadily more conservative as social status diminished. The blue-collar working class is not as well represented by labor's political activity than the upper crust of union membership, and therefore the blue-collar worker provides more fertile territory for Republicans and conservatives than their wealthier and better educated counterparts.

Following is a table comparing the responses of different status categories for selected questions:

Table 59. Attitudes By Occupation

	Upper White-Collar	Lower White-Collar	Upper Blue-Collar	Lower Blue-Collar
Defense Spending				
Increase	25.0	34.8	36.2	30.8
Unsure	17.0	17.8	20.4	20.9
Decrease	58.0	47.4	43.4	48.4
Budget Policy: Dislike				
Raise Federal Income Taxes	28.6	31.6	36.4	37.4
Cut Federal Programs and Services	32.7	27.4	25.6	26.8
Continue to Borrow Money	35.2	38.9	34.3	32.5
Don't Know/No Answer	3.6	2.1	3.7	3.3
Domestic Content: First Question				
Favor	60.6	68.9	82.5	84.1
Unsure	11.4	14.1	4.0	3.8
Oppose	28.0	17.0	13.5	12.1
Domestic Content: Follow-up **(asked of those who favored)**				
Still Favor (as a percentage of *total* sample)	50.4	58.5	69.0	68.7
Now Oppose (as a percentage of *total* sample)	10.2	10.4	13.5	15.4
Tuition Tax Credits				
Favor	38.6	51.9	44.5	50.5
Unsure	5.3	8.1	5.5	7.7
Oppose	56.1	40.0	50.0	41.8
Amnesty				
Favor	42.9	42.1	39.7	33.3
Unsure	12.2	16.8	5.0	10.6
Oppose	44.9	41.1	55.4	56.1

	Upper White-Collar	Lower White-Collar	Upper Blue-Collar	Lower Blue-Collar
Ronald Reagan				
Approve Strongly	15.5	22.2	26.4	22.0
Approve	24.2	17.8	15.8	17.6
Undecided	8.3	12.6	11.2	10.4
Disapprove	10.2	14.8	10.6	10.4
Disapprove Strongly	40.2	32.6	35.1	39.6
Don't know/no answer	1.5	0.0	0.9	0.0
Jesse Jackson				
Never Heard of	1.1	0.7	2.0	1.6
Heard of only	2.3	3.0	2.6	5.5
Know/Favorable	51.1	43.7	36.8	36.3
Know/Unfavorable	25.8	31.1	36.8	33.5
Know/No Opinion	19.7	21.5	21.8	23.1
Comparable Worth: First Question				
Favor	91.3	91.9	87.1	83.6
Unsure	2.3	2.2	2.3	4.4
Oppose	6.4	5.9	10.6	12.1
Comparable Worth: Follow-up **(asked of those who favored)**				
Still Favor (as a percentage of *total* sample)	62.5	56.3	48.0	45.1
Now Oppose (as a percentage of *total* sample)	28.8	35.6	39.1	38.5
Personal Ideology				
Very Conservative	6.1	8.9	11.2	14.3
Somewhat Conservative	37.9	40.7	45.4	41.2
Moderate	6.4	8.9	5.2	8.2
Somewhat Liberal	42.8	31.1	30.7	30.2
Very Liberal	6.8	10.4	7.5	6.0
Reagan vs. Mondale				
Reagan	29.6	34.3	35.6	37.6
Unsure	20.0	14.9	11.0	19.8
Mondale	50.4	50.7	53.4	42.6
Union Leadership Represents my Views				
Agree	36.7	32.6	33.9	30.8
Unsure	7.6	8.9	7.8	7.7
Disagree	55.7	58.5	58.3	61.5

Chapter 5
Conclusion

Organized labor is indisputably a significant and influential force in American politics. Its endorsement often brings political candidates substantial assistance, both in the form of campaign contributions and in the form of manpower and expertise. While support from organized labor can sometimes bring with it the negative baggage associated with the image of a controversial institution, its support is generally considered a net plus. After all, while John Glenn and Gary Hart both sought to use the AFL-CIO endorsement against Walter Mondale, both originally sought that endorsement for themselves. And of course, whatever the baggage, it was Walter Mondale who won his party's nomination.

But support from organized labor for an issue or a candidate has long been presumed to carry something more than simply money and expertise and volunteers. It was often assumed that there was a correlation between the official positions of the unions and the voting behavior of their members—perhaps because leadership was guided by membership opinions when formulating policy, or perhaps because membership was guided by leadership positions when they entered the voting booths.

The presidential election of 1980—in which most union leaders strongly preferred the Democratic nominee, only to see so many of their members supporting his successful challenger—suggested that membership is capable of quite a bit of independence. Numerous questions in our poll demonstrated that there are important issues on which rank and file opinions—particularly blue-collar rank and file positions—are not in line with official union policy. This disparity was most obvious when we compared the views of the activists in our sample to the views of the non-activists: the activists were almost always significantly to the left.

It is not that we found a right-of-center consensus among the rank and file. It is rather that—with the exception of a few issues, like domestic content and comparable worth—we found a complete absence of any left-of-center consensus. Labor votes are available to those political candidates with the energy and foresight to frame the proper issues and go after the appropriate segments of the working population. The one area of questions over which we discovered a consensus was that dealing with attitudes by union members towards their unions, and it revealed the surprisingly deep disenchantment and alienation felt by union members toward their leadership and its political activities. Political candidates cannot consign working men and women to union leadership, on the assumption that they are a voting bloc that can be brokered and delivered. Such a view fails to capture the diversity of working class attitudes, and is thus both deeply patronizing and politically unwise. The Democratic Party has a strong hold on the allegiance of the leadership of organized labor. The test over the next several years will be over which party—and which philosophy—can win the allegiance of those that refuse to be led.

Appendix
Nationwide Union Study Methodology

The basic sample for the Nationwide Union Study was a full national probability sample of all telephone households in the continental United States. This sample was generated using random digit dialing techniques (RDD) in order to ensure the inclusion of unlisted phone numbers.

A labor union membership screen was used for each contacted household. Union membership was thus self-reported by each interviewed respondent. Interviews were completed with union members only. Non-union households were terminated. One interview was completed in each union household. One thousand (N=1000) interviews were completed.

A strict random selection device was used to control the sex composition of this sample. In households with only one union member, or in which all union members were of the same sex, an interview was completed with that sex respondent. In households in which there were at least two union members, and in which there was at least one union member of each sex, a random selection device was used to select which sex union member was interviewed. The resulting sex distribution—63% male, 37% female—should therefore approximate the sex distribution of the population of union members in this country.

The initial first phase sample of N=702 interviews was not stratified by geography. This sample was *self-weighting by geography*, and thus reflects the distribution of union households across the continental United States.

The final 298 interviews in this study were based on a modified cluster sampling procedure. A sample of 298 of the originally completed 702 interviews was selected randomly. The phone exchange (area code, central office code, and first two digits of the phone number stem) from each of these 298 completed interviews was then used as a cluster point from which additional phone numbers were randomly generated. One additional interview was then completed in each cluster.

It should be pointed out that the national and international union membership as self-reported by the union members themselves in this national survey included approximately 50 separate union designations. Additionally, approximately 17% of the union national sample came from education and school-oriented unions. Other union designations included: United Auto Workers (7%), Teamsters (7%), United Steel Workers (3%), Communication Workers of America (3%), United Mine Workers (1%), the Musicians Union, and even the Writers and Screen Actors Guild. When the various union designations were regrouped, they were categorized into the following substructures:

AFL-CIO	55%
Teamsters	8%
Education/schools	17%
Government	8%
Miscellaneous	8%
Refused	6%

Although many educators are also government employees, with many of them members of the AFL-CIO, we did not count them twice.

The survey was conducted between April 5 and April 15, 1984 by V. Lance Tarrance & Associates of Houston, Texas for the Institute for Government and Politics. The total sample includes 1,000 union members. The margin of error for the total 1,000 sample is approximately ± 3.1%. For subsamples of 500, the margin of error is 4.5%. The survey was directed by Dr. Frank Newport of Tarrance & Associates and Dr. Stuart Rothenberg of the Institute for Government and Politics.

Notes

Introduction

1. Del Marth, "The Sorry State of Unions," *Nation's Business* (July, 1982): 51.
2. Quoted in Seligman, "Who Needs Unions?", *Fortune* (July 12, 1982): 54.
3. Lance Compa, "Hard Choices," *Progressive* (January, 1982): 29.
4. Michael Jackson, *Trade Unions* (London: Longman, 1982), p. 5.
5. Graham K. Wilson, *Unions in American National Politics* (London: Macmillan, 1979), p. 14.
6. "Labor's Downcast Labor Day," *Time* (September 13, 1982): 72.
7. "Are Unions Dead or Just Sleeping?" (Panel Discussion), *Fortune* (September 20, 1982): 98.
8. Kathy Sawyer, "Unions Beleaguered by Demons of Change", *Washington Post* (September 11, 1983): 13.
9. Del Marth, "The Sorry State of Unions," *Nation's Business* (July, 1982): 50.
10. Del Marth, "Why Unions Lose at Many Companies," *Nation's Business* (August, 1982): 50.
11. Kathy Sawyer, "Unions Beleaguered by Demons of Change", *Washington Post* (September 11, 1983): 13.
12. *Congressional Record*, February 17, 1976, S 1660-1662.
13. "FEC Publishes Final 1981-82 PAC Study," Press Release, Federal Election Commission, November 19, 1983.
14. Del Marth, "The Sorry State of Unions," p. 51.

Chapter 1

1. "Democrats Pressed on Platform Keyed to Full Employment," *AFL-CIO News* (March 31, 1984): 1.
2. "Kirkland Cites Challenges Facing Labor", *AFL-CIO News* (December 20, 1983).
3. "Mondale Makes Fairness a Key Campaign Issue," *AFL-CIO News* (March 24, 1984): 1.
4. *AFL-CIO News* (January 21, 1984): 6-7.
5. "Balanced Budget Amendment First on Senate's Schedule," *AFL-CIO News* (July 10, 1982): 2.
6. "Council Warns Reagan Policies Pose Long-Term Economic Peril," *AFL-CIO News* (February 25, 1984): 1.
7. "Where America's Unions Go From Here" (Interview), *U.S. News & World Report* (May 17, 1982): 71-73.
8. "Business Blames Reagan Recession on Federal Deficit, but Lobbies to Keep Their Tax Windfall," *AFL-CIO News* (July 3, 1982): 8.
9. "Kirkland Cites Challenges Facing Labor," *AFL-CIO News* (December 20, 1983).
10. Willis Witter, "UAW Drive Backs Bill to Require Use of U.S. Parts," *Washington Times* (July 13, 1982).
11. "Domestic Content Bill Wins House Approval," *AFL-CIO News* (December 18, 1982).

12. Wilson, *op. cit.*, p. 127.
13. "Detente," Congressional Hearings—Senate Committee on Foreign Relations, 93rd Congress, 2nd Session, 1974.
14. "Where America's Unions Go From Here," *U.S. News & World Report* (May 17, 1982): 72.
15. *Wall Street Journal* (June 28, 1983).
16. Lance Compa, "Breaking Ranks," *Progressive* (June, 1982): 36.
17. Herbert Hill, "The Racial Practices of Organized Labor," in Arthur M. Ross and Herbert Hill, ed., *Employment, Race and Poverty* (NY: Harcourt Brace & World, 1967).
18. Sterling Spero and Abram Harris, *The Black Worker* (NY: Kennikat Press, Inc. 1931): 477-78.
19. Walter Williams, *The State Against Blacks* (N.Y.: McGraw-Hill, 1982): 99-108.
20. Paul Magnusson, "Jackson Campaign Woos Black Unionists," *Detroit Free Press* (January 22, 1984): 7A.
21. Wilson, *op. cit.*, p. 72.
22. *Id.*, p. 46.
23. "The Civil Rights Retreat," *AFL-CIO News* (January 21, 1984): 15.
24. "Democrats Pressed on Platform Keyed to Full Employment," *AFL-CIO News* (March 31, 1984).
25. "Labor, Civil Right Ties Stressed by Kirkland," *AFL-CIO News* (February 18, 1984): 2.
26. Magnusson, *op. cit.*
27. "Labor Women Supported in Equity Battle," *AFL-CIO News* (January 28, 1984): 3.
28. "AFSCME Warns Pay Equity Could Become Election Issue," *AFL-CIO News* (February 11, 1984).
29. James Ridgeway, "Inside the Political Theatre," *Village Voice* (July 24, 1984).

Chapter 2

1. Carolyn Barta, "Powers of Organized Labor," *Dallas Morning News* (May 23, 1983): H1.
2. "Labor Letter," *Wall Street Journal* (January 24, 1984): 1.
3. "COPE's Political Craftsmen Build Smooth Organization," *National Journal* (September 12, 1980): 1969-79.
4. Wilson, *op. cit.*, p. 20.
5. *Id.*, p. 21.
6. *Free Trade Union News* (April 1966).
7. *Evening Star* (May 5, 1955): 28.
8. Wilson, *op. cit.*, p. 28.
9. "Perkins Stresses Political Independence," *AFL-CIO News* (July 13, 1982): 5.
10. "FEC Publishes Final 1981-82 PAC Study," Press Release, Federal Election Commission, November 19, 1983.
11. Wilson, *op. cit.*, p. 27.
12. Lance Compa, "Hard Choices," *Progressive* (January, 1982): 27.
13. *AFL-CIO News* (July 31, 1982): 8.
14. Lance Compa, "Hard Choices," *Progressive* (January, 1982): 29.
15. Michael Jackson, *op. cit.*, p. 127.
16. William Keller, "Reagan to Bypass Union Leaders in his Quest for Members Votes," *New York Times* (July 2, 1984): 1.
17. *AFL-CIO News* (February 18, 1984).

18. NBC Nightly News, June 24, 1984.
19. *Id.*
20. *Id.*
21. *Id.*
22. Kathy Sawyer, "Organized Labor Attempts to Gauge Damage to Mondale, Itself," *Washington Post* (March 1, 1984): A8.
23. *Id.*
24. *Id.*
25. William Keller, *op. cit.*
26. "Poll In Michigan Finds Majority Prefer Reagan," *New York Times* (June 26, 1984).

Chapter 3

1. Kathy Sawyer, "Lane Kirkland: Made in America," *Washington Post* (July 15, 1984): K1.